DATE DUE

GENES & DISEASE

PARKINSON'S DISEASE

GENES & DISEASE

Alzheimer's Disease

Asthma

Cystic Fibrosis

Diabetes

Down Syndrome

Hemophilia

Huntington's Disease

Parkinson's Disease

Sickle Cell Disease

Tay-Sachs Disease

GENES & DISEASE

PARKINSON'S DISEASE

Natalie Goldstein

An imprint of Infobase Publishing

Parkinson's Disease

Copyright © 2009 by Infobase Publishing

Chelsea House
An imprint of Infobase Publishing
132 West 31st Street
New York NY 10001

Library of Congress Cataloging-in-Publication Data

Goldstein, Natalie.
  Parkinson's disease / Natalie Goldstein.
    p. cm. — (Genes and disease)
  Includes bibliographical references and index.
  ISBN 978-0-7910-9584-3 (hardcover)
  1. Parkinson's disease—Popular works. I. Title. II. Series.
  RC382.G65 2008
  616.8'33—dc22   2008010494

Chelsea House books are available at special discounts when purchased in bulk quantities for businesses, associations, institutions, or sales promotions. Please call our Special Sales Department in New York at (212) 967-8800 or (800) 322-8755.

You can find Chelsea House on the World Wide Web at
http://www.chelseahouse.com

Text design by Annie O'Donnell
Cover design by Ben Peterson

Printed in the United States of America

Bang NMSG 10 9 8 7 6 5 4 3 2 1

This book is printed on acid-free paper.

All links and Web addresses were checked and verified to be correct at the time of publication. Because of the dynamic nature of the Web, some addresses and links may have changed since publication and may no longer be valid.

CONTENTS

1

THE TREMBLING
WAS THE MESSAGE

The movie star with the irresistible boyish grin had been partying long and hard the night before. It had been a late night. He had had too much to drink. He was making a movie in Florida and was working—and playing—very long hours. So when he woke up and discovered an odd "message," he shrugged it off. "I woke up to find the message in my left hand. It had me trembling. It wasn't a fax, telegram, memo, or the usual sort of missive [letter] bringing disturbing news. In fact, my hand held nothing at all. The trembling [in the pinkie of my hand] was the message."[1]

One of his first thoughts was, "Weird—maybe I slept on it funny."[2] But the trembling in actor Michael J. Fox's left hand did not go away, no matter what he did. All day, then day after day, his left hand trembled. Try as he might, the actor could think of nothing he had done that would have caused this strange shaking. It was only later, when his symptoms could no longer be ignored, that Michael J. Fox was forced to confront what he had first discovered on the morning of November 13, 1990.

That morning, my brain was serving notice; it had initiated a divorce from my mind. Efforts to contest or reconcile would be futile; eighty percent of the process, I

FIGURE 1.1 Michael J. Fox, a popular actor, was diagnosed with Parkinson's disease when he was only 29 years old.

would later learn, was already complete. No grounds were given, and the petition was irrevocable. Further, my brain was demanding, and incrementally seizing, custody of my body, beginning with the baby; the outermost finger of my left hand.[3]

In September 1991, Michael J. Fox received his initial diagnosis of **Parkinson's disease**. At first, he could not believe it. Surely, he thought, Parkinson's disease only affects the elderly. Fox was not yet 30 years old when his first symptoms appeared. He saw other doctors who, he was convinced, would see that "this whole Parkinson's thing has been a colossal mistake."[4] When a **neurologist**, a nervous system specialist, who specialized in Parkinson's confirmed the diagnosis in October of that year, Fox had to come to terms with the undeniable fact that he had the disease.

WHAT IS PARKINSON'S DISEASE?

Michael J. Fox was right in thinking that Parkinson's disease is an illness that mainly strikes older people. In fact, the average age for the onset of Parkinson's disease is 60. More than 80% of people who develop Parkinson's disease are diagnosed when they are between 40 and 70 years old.

Parkinson's disease is quite common in the United States. About 1.2 million Americans have Parkinson's disease, and about 50,000 new cases are diagnosed every year.[5] Medical experts expect the number of Parkinson's cases to increase in the next couple of decades. There are two reasons for this. First, people are living longer. Today, life expectancy is 77.2 years, up from 50 years in 1900.[6] Second, the huge population of baby boomers (Americans born between 1945 and about 1965) is approaching the age at which Parkinson's appears. Together, these two factors almost guarantee that the number of Parkinson's patients is set to increase.

In a small number of cases, Parkinson's disease strikes younger people. About 5% of Parkinson's cases occur in people between 30 and 40 years of age. Michael J. Fox was diagnosed with Parkinson's disease when he was only 29 years old. His doctors told him that he had likely had the disease for years before his symptoms first appeared. So Fox was unusually young for a Parkinson's sufferer.

Parkinson's disease is first and foremost a disease affecting the nervous system, particularly the brain. One part of the brain contains special nerve cells that produce a chemical that controls the body's movement. In Parkinson's disease, these nerve cells become damaged and die, so less of this movement-controlling chemical is produced.

Parkinson's disease is classified as a movement disorder because it affects how the body moves. There are two types of movement disorders. One type causes excess movement or activity. The second type slows or prevents movement. Parkinson's disease is in the second category.

Parkinson's disease is not contagious. People cannot "catch" Parkinson's the way they can catch a cold. Chapter 4 will explore the factors that can cause Parkinson's disease. Parkinson's is a chronic disease, which means that people who get it will have it their whole lives. However, there are treatments that help relieve the disease's symptoms. Parkinson's is also a progressively degenerative disease. *Progressively* means "increasing over time." *Degenerative* means "declining in quality." A progressively degenerative disease is thus one that gets continually worse. Over time, the disease causes an ever-worsening decline in the functioning of the nervous system. As more brain cells become damaged and die, the symptoms of Parkinson's get worse.

The first symptom of Parkinson's disease is usually **involuntary** movement or trembling of a body part, also called **tremors**. Tremors result from a lack of the controlling chemical in the brain. As Parkinson's progresses, new symptoms appear. One common symptom of Parkinson's disease is muscle stiffness, also called **rigidity**. As time passes, a person with Parkinson's disease may also experience poor balance, lack of coordination (such as eye-hand coordination), slowed movements, and changes in posture.

Diagnosing Parkinson's disease can be very tricky. That is because there are other, often less serious conditions that may look a lot like Parkinson's, but are not. For example, older people sometimes have shaky hands. Very often, shaky hands are a symptom of a condition called *essential tremor*, which is a less serious disease. It may take a

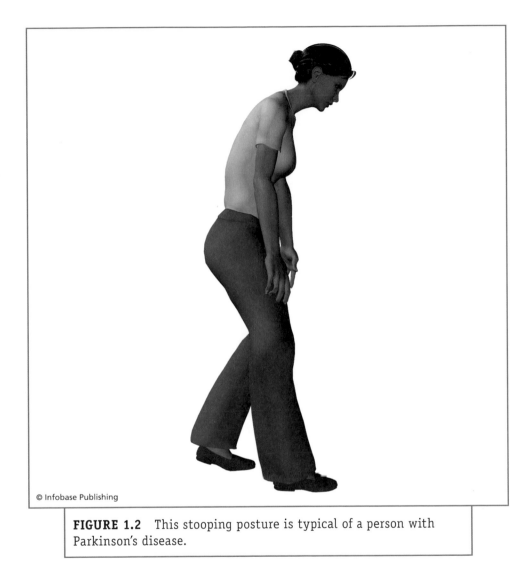

© Infobase Publishing

FIGURE 1.2 This stooping posture is typical of a person with Parkinson's disease.

neurologist several months of repeated evaluations before a patient is diagnosed with Parkinson's disease.

One of the most important things a neurologist must do is talk to the patient. Getting a complete medical—and life—history helps the neurologist make a correct diagnosis.

That is because there are many factors that may produce symptoms similar to Parkinson's disease. For example, sometimes a person may be taking medication for another condition. The medication may have a side effect that causes tremor. In some cases, people who are long-time heavy drinkers of alcoholic beverages may develop shaky hands or other types of tremor. There are even cases in which a brain injury—such as a severe blow to the head—may cause Parkinson's-like tremors. The different conditions that sometimes mimic Parkinson's disease are discussed in detail later in this book. The neurologist must know about these and other things before he or she can make a diagnosis of Parkinson's disease.

PARKINSON'S DISEASE OR ESSENTIAL TREMOR?

Essential tremor is a movement disorder, one of a number of conditions that cause trembling in the body. Essential tremor often begins with shaking in the hands. In essential tremor, the hands shake when they are moving or doing something. This is the opposite of Parkinson's disease, in which the hands often shake when they are at rest (though they can shake at any time). Another way that essential tremor differs from Parkinson's is that essential tremor sometimes begins with shaking of the head or with a trembling voice. These symptoms rarely occur in patients first diagnosed with Parkinson's disease.

Like Parkinson's disease, essential tremor is chronic and gets progressively worse. However, its symptoms usually do not become as serious as those of Parkinson's disease. Essential tremor is also far more common than Parkinson's. About 6 million people in the United States suffer from essential tremor.[7]

Parkinson's is a serious disease, but it is not a death sentence. Although there is currently no cure for Parkinson's, it can be treated. With proper treatment, a person with Parkinson's may be able to live a happy and productive life for many years.

2

A SHORT HISTORY OF PARKINSON'S DISEASE

Early in the nineteenth century, English physician James Parkinson was talking with a fellow doctor. His colleague had come across a man who had an unusual and mysterious condition. The doctor told Parkinson that this man, a 50-year-old gardener, was having a difficult time working because he could not stop the shaking in his left hand and arm. The poor man was afraid that he would lose his only means of supporting himself and his family. The gardener visited Parkinson's colleague, who questioned him about his condition. Neither the gardener nor the doctor could figure out what was causing his problem.

The mysterious case aroused Parkinson's professional curiosity. He went to see the gardener to find out for himself what type of condition he had. Parkinson, too, was at a loss about what to do to help the gardener. However, Parkinson decided that he would study this condition to discover its cause and, hopefully, its treatment.

Parkinson conducted a highly unusual study of what he and the physicians of that time called *paralysis agitans*, or shaking palsy. He investigated the condition by walking the streets of London, looking for people who had the symptoms of shaking palsy. He talked to each sufferer he met and wrote down the story of each person's life up to and including the onset of their disease. In some cases, he invited them back to his office so he could examine them. Here, Parkinson describes one person he encountered.

> The subject . . . was met casually in the street. [He] was a man sixty-two years of age; the greater part of whose life had been spent as an attendant at a [judge's] office. He had suffered from the disease about eight or ten years. All [his limbs] were considerably agitated, [his] speech was very much interrupted, and [his] body much bowed and shaken. He walked almost entirely on the fore part of his feet, and would have fallen every step if he had not been supported by his stick. He described the disease as having come on very gradually. . . . He was [now] the inmate of a poor-house, . . . and being fully assured of the incurable nature of his complaint, declined making any attempt for relief.[8]

One sufferer Parkinson met looked like he once had been fit and athletic, but the 65-year-old man had a severe stoop and could "walk" only by running. This man, like many others, reported to Parkinson that his condition appeared gradually and worsened slowly over time. Another elderly man whom Parkinson saw only from a distance was able to walk only with a hand on each shoulder of a helper who supported him. Even so, the man moved at a run, had a very stooped posture, and rocked back and forth continuously.

Parkinson observed and listened to many people and gathered an enormous amount of information about their condition. He then spent a good deal of time thinking about the information he had gathered about shaking palsy. After carefully analyzing all the information, Parkinson decided to publish a report about his findings. His report was titled "An Essay on the Shaking Palsy," and it was published in London in 1817.

Parkinson's report is important for several reasons. First, he made a detailed analysis of the symptoms reported by the ailing people he interviewed. Second, he was able to classify these symptoms to show that different symptoms were particular to different diseases; that is, not everyone who had shaking palsy had the same disease. Parkinson would show that some people actually had epilepsy or other medical conditions—some even had tremors caused by drinking too much alcohol. Finally, Parkinson described the symptoms—and their gradual onset—that characterized what he believed was true shaking palsy. His careful analysis helped doctors make a correct diagnosis of the disease that came to bear his name—Parkinson's disease. Parkinson described the disease as having the following characteristic symptoms: "Involuntary tremulous motion, with lessened muscular power, in parts not in action and even when supported; with a propensity to bend the trunk forward, and to pass from a walking to a running pace; the senses and the intellect being uninjured."[9]

Parkinson admitted that his study was informal and incomplete, based as it was on a relatively limited number of cases. However, his paper is considered a classic in medicine because nearly all of his descriptions of the disease have turned out to be correct. Parkinson accurately described the sequence of symptoms: initial tremor in a limb, then increasingly stooped posture and difficulty walking, and increasing loss of muscle control.

As often happens, James Parkinson's important research was ignored for decades. In the mid-1800s, a French physician, Jean-Martin Charcot, became interested in shaking palsy and began to research the disease. He found and read Parkinson's report. Charcot was impressed by Parkinson's work, and he expanded on it. Charcot is credited with recognizing that muscle rigidity is a key symptom of this disease.

He therefore rejected the term "shaking palsy." Instead, he named the condition Parkinson's disease in honor of James Parkinson.

TREMORS THROUGH TIME

Though James Parkinson first described the disease that bears his name in the nineteenth century, it is very likely that Parkinson's disease has afflicted humanity for thousands of years. Medical historians have pored over ancient records and concluded that Parkinson's disease was known a long time ago.

One of the first descriptions of what was probably a case of Parkinson's disease was found in India in ancient Sanskrit writings from about 4,500 years ago. An ancient Egyptian papyrus text dating to 1350 B.C. also contains a description of a disease closely resembling Parkinson's. In the second century A.D., the great Greek physician Galen made a study of people suffering from tremors. Galen is the first physician known to distinguish different types of tremors; for example, tremors that occur when the limb or body is at rest and tremors that occur during activity.

In the fifteenth century, during the Renaissance, the great Italian artist Leonardo da Vinci recorded his observations of people "who tremble without permission of the soul."[10] Later, the seventeenth-century artist Rembrandt created a famous etching titled "The Good Samaritan," in which one character is shown stooped, with his hands in the thumbs-touching, trembling position typical of Parkinson's disease.

Physicians practicing during these times, before true scientific advances in medicine, continued to study trembling diseases and offer their suggestions about what caused them. In the mid-1700s, German doctor Johann Juncker confirmed Galen's description of the two types of tremors.

However, Juncker suggested that active tremors were caused by strong emotional reactions, such as extreme fear or anger. He had no explanation for resting tremors except old age. Around the same time, the French physician François Boissier de Sauvages described the way some patients could maintain their balance only by walking quickly or running.

Such was the limited state of medical knowledge about this condition when James Parkinson conducted his invaluable study. Parkinson's work was immensely important in advancing understanding about this disease. Yet Parkinson himself admitted that his conclusions were, in effect, mere speculation. Gaining a true understanding of this disease awaited the scientific exploration of the human nervous system.

THE BRAIN (PARTLY) REVEALED

By the middle of the nineteenth century, many physicians were working to find the cause of Parkinson's disease. They had limited tools available to them, and so their findings were maddeningly off the mark. Some physicians looked at the **spinal cord** to see if it showed signs of disease. It did not. Other scientists pursued the notion that the cause of Parkinson's disease was to be found in the muscles. It was not there, either. Researchers of the day became so frustrated that they began referring to Parkinson's disease as a "neurosis," a condition having no known cause in the physical structure of the nervous system.

The second half of the nineteenth century saw important advances in the understanding of human **anatomy**. Many physicians dissected human corpses to learn about body organs and cells. Much of this new knowledge was aided by the more sophisticated tools available to scientists at that time. Better microscopes, for example, permitted scientists

THE REAL "BODY SNATCHERS"

In the early 1800s, Edinburgh, Scotland, was famous for the availability of fine medical education, especially in human anatomy. At that time, doctors studied anatomy by dissecting the corpses of criminals who had been executed by hanging. Anatomy schools became so popular in Edinburgh that there were soon too few executed criminals to serve as teaching tools.

As economists tell us, if there is a demand for something, someone will find a way to fulfill it. To make up for the shortage of dead criminals, there arose a booming business in grave robbing. Grave robbers, also called resurrection men, haunted cemeteries to locate the recently deceased. **Anatomists** needed fresh—not decayed—bodies, so the grave robbers had to find newly buried bodies to dig up. The grave robbers became so adept at their craft that they could open a grave, remove a body, and replace the disturbed soil in just a few minutes. Doctors paid handsomely for the delivery of a fresh corpse—usually in the middle of the night. Physicians rarely asked questions about where the body came from.

William Burke and William Hare were two of the most notorious grave robbers. When finding fresh graves became too difficult, they decided to "create" their own fresh corpses. The two men found their marks in seedy pubs. First, they got their victim drunk. Then the two "businessmen" murdered the victim and sold the extremely fresh (often still warm) body to a doctor, particularly one Dr. Knox. By the time they were caught in 1829, Burke and Hare had murdered 16 people and sold their bodies to anatomists. It was never discovered how many dead bodies they and their fellow resurrection men had taken out of graves.

(continues)

(continued)

The British government put an end to grave robbing in 1832 with the passage of the Anatomy Act. The act guaranteed physicians an abundance of corpses because it made legally available the unclaimed bodies of the destitute who died in poorhouses.

to see individual cells and even the tiny **organelles** inside them. Autopsies revealed that the human brain was made up of many different parts, though exactly what those parts did was still a mystery.

In the late 1800s, Italian anatomist Camillo Golgi developed a stain that allowed physicians to study in detail the structure of nerve cells, or **neurons**. Golgi's studies revealed that the brain is made up of billions of individual microscopic neurons, each containing a cell body with a **nucleus** and other organelles, as well as many long, thin, threadlike extensions. While Golgi studied neurons, Edouard Brissaud, one of Charcot's students, was learning about the many different parts of the human brain. Brissaud suggested that a small, black-tinted nerve center in the **brain stem**, called the **substantia nigra**, might be related to Parkinson's disease. Brissaud had done many autopsies on people who had had Parkinson's symptoms. He observed that these people had minute differences in this region of the brain.

In 1919, a French medical student named Constantin Tretiakoff was working on his doctoral thesis at a Paris medical school. Tretiakoff found that abnormalities in the substantia nigra were always associated with Parkinson's disease. These changes included loss of the darkly pigmented nerve

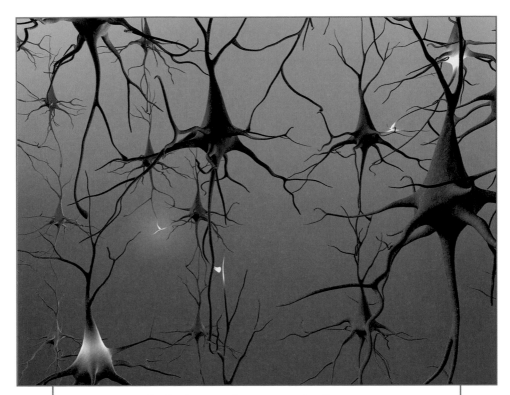

FIGURE 2.1   The brain contains a network of neurons, or nerve cells. Nerve cells have long extensions that help them carry messages to different parts of the body.

cells in the substantia nigra and the presence of unusual round objects that were absent in people who did not have Parkinson's. These odd, spherical objects had been identified and studied a few years before by another physician, Frederick H. Lewy. In 1912, Lewy published a paper in which he reported finding these strange objects in the brain cells of more than 75% of Parkinson's sufferers. Healthy brains did not contain these bodies, which became known as **Lewy** (pronounced lah-VEY) **bodies**.

The new findings were interesting, but not very enlightening. The questions remained: What did the substantia nigra do? What causes the abnormalities in the substantia nigra? What does the presence of Lewy bodies signify? How do both of these findings relate to Parkinson's disease? It took decades before anyone could answer these questions.

The pursuit of answers to these questions was put on hold during World War II, when most doctors were understandably more concerned with treating injured soldiers than with this type of research. However, after the war, research picked up once again, and improvements in technology allowed scientists better access to the secrets of the brain. In the 1950s, Swedish biologist Arvid Carlsson and his team of researchers developed a new technique for staining cells. The new staining method permitted biologists to study cells in greater detail than ever before. Using this technique, biologists could directly observe and study the substantia nigra and other vital parts of the brain. The Swedish researchers made a monumental discovery about the function of the substantia nigra. They found that this part of the brain normally produces large quantities of a vital chemical that carries messages to the **corpus striatum**, the part of the brain that controls body movement, balance, and walking. The crucial chemical these researchers discovered is called **dopamine**. The discovery of dopamine revolutionized the understanding and treatment of Parkinson's disease.

3

THE BRAIN AND PARKINSON'S DISEASE

The brain is the most amazing and complex organ in the human body. It is the organ that regulates every function to maintain the harmony and health of the body. Normally, people are not aware of being "regulated," because the brain does its job perfectly. The brain is the command center of the **central nervous system**, or CNS, which also includes the spinal cord that runs down the back and the nerves that extend from the spinal cord to every part of the body. Messages to and from the brain are carried by the nerves and spinal cord to and from all parts of the body. By responding to orders from the brain, the CNS controls the body's functions

Before delving into what goes wrong in a malfunctioning brain, it is important to understand how a well-functioning brain works. This chapter will not cover every part or every function of the brain—that would take up volumes. Instead, it focuses on those parts and functions of the brain that are related to Parkinson's disease.

THE MAIN PARTS OF THE BRAIN

The brain is made up of about 100 billion neurons, or nerve cells, and it sits within the skull, the bony structure that surrounds and protects it. The **cerebrum** is the largest part of the brain and is the part that enables people to think, decide, remember, and learn. It also helps control body movement. Most of these functions are controlled by the **cerebral cortex**, the outermost layer of the brain, which sends and receives messages to and from the body and other parts of the brain.

The outer surface of the cerebral cortex is marked by ridges and grooves, or *convolutions*, that increase its surface area. The cerebral cortex is made up of several regions, each dedicated to sending and receiving messages that have to do with specific functions. For example, the region called the frontal lobe has two main functions. One function is to control voluntary movement, including movements associated with speech. Voluntary movement is carried out by **voluntary muscle**, muscle that can be moved at will. The second function of the frontal lobe is to act as the center that controls emotional expression and moral and ethical behavior. The region of the cerebral cortex behind the frontal lobe is called the parietal lobe. It controls the processing of visual images and the ability to recognize objects.

The **cerebellum** is the part of the brain that coordinates movement of skeletal muscles, the voluntary muscles that are connected to bones. The cerebellum sends and receives messages to and from the body's muscles, tendons, and joints. It is also communicates with the inner ear, and thus controls balance.

The brain stem is the lower part of the brain that connects with the spinal cord. The brain stem contains many structures that are vital to keeping people alive. These structures control what is called the **autonomic nervous system**—the nervous system that functions independently of a person's will or thoughts. For example, breathing and heartbeat are controlled by structures in the brain stem.

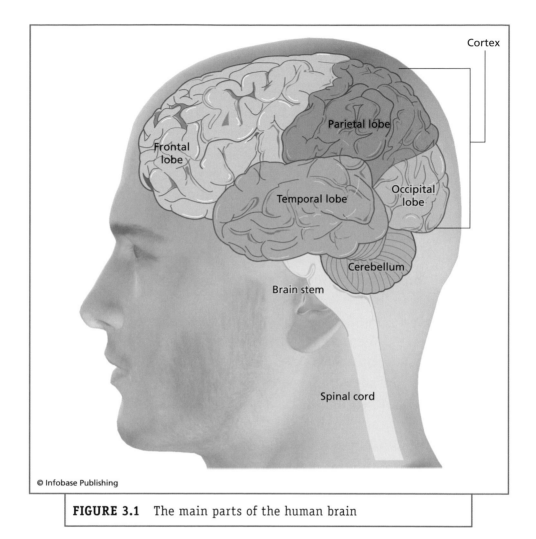

© Infobase Publishing

FIGURE 3.1 The main parts of the human brain

NERVE CELLS AND COMMUNICATION

Neurons have a unique shape and function. A neuron is a long, thin cell. Extending from one end are **dendrites**, branching receptors that receive messages called **impulses** from other neurons and carry them toward the cell body. The cell body is a broader area that contains the nucleus and organelles. Emerging from the other end of the cell body is a long, thin fiber called the **axon**. Impulses pass from the cell body down the axon to the **axon terminals**.

An impulse is a small electrical and chemical signal that travels quickly along the membrane that surrounds the nerve cell. Impulses pass along neurons in one direction, from the dendrites to the cell body and then along the axon. At the end of the axon is a gap called the **synapse**, which is a space between the end of the axon of one neuron and the dendrites of the next neuron. The passage of impulses across the synapse is accomplished with special chemicals called **neurotransmitters**. There are many different kinds of neurotransmitters, which have specific functions in different parts of the nervous system.

When an impulse reaches the axon terminals, it causes the release of neurotransmitters into the synapse, the gap between neurons. The neurotransmitter crosses the synapse and initiates impulses in the dendrites of the next neuron. Each neuron has thousands of dendrites and axon terminals.

Although the passage of impulses from one neuron to the next across a gap may seem like an inefficient and time-consuming process, it takes place almost instantaneously. In the instant it takes to wiggle a big toe, a signal travels from the brain to the toe muscles and "instructs" them to wiggle. That is quick communication.

A neuron's dendrites are like light switches because they can receive two different types of signals—on or off. About 1,000 times per second, dendrites monitor incoming neurotransmitters from other nerve cells. The dendrites "add up" the number of "on" chemical signals and the number of "off" chemical signals they get. If the dendrites get more "off" than "on" signals, then the cell is not activated. If they get more "on" than "off" signals, the neuron is activated. The

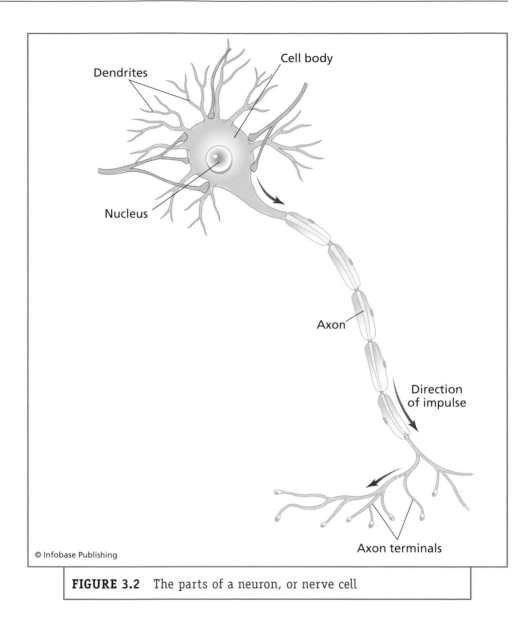

FIGURE 3.2 The parts of a neuron, or nerve cell

activated neuron sends impulses down the axon to the axon terminals, which produce their particular neurotransmitter. The chemical is released and travels across the synapse to nearby nerve cells. Actually, since each neuron is connected to about 10,000 other neurons, the chemical message is sent to all of them. Each neuron "fires" a signal (on or off) 10,000 times each second, so it is easy to see how quickly and widely signals are received and sent.

THE HEALTHY BRAIN

Different structures in the brain release different neurotransmitters. Remember that a neurotransmitter is a chemical, and different chemicals have different properties. It might help to think of the neurotransmitter's properties in terms of shape. The neurotransmitter released by one type of brain neuron has a particular shape—say, a

DOPAMINE

Neurons in the substantia nigra make the neurotransmitter dopamine out of **tyrosine**, an **amino acid.** Amino acids are a class of molecules that are the building blocks of proteins. Converting tyrosine to dopamine involves two steps. In step one, an **enzyme** chemically alters the tyrosine to make a compound called **levodopa**, or **L-dopa**. In step two, another enzyme changes the L-dopa into dopamine.

The movie *Awakenings* (1990), which starred Robin Williams and Robert DeNiro, was based on a true story written by neurologist Oliver Sacks in his 1973 book of the same name. In this movie, Dr. Oliver Sacks (Robin Williams) treats hospital patients, including Robert DeNiro's character, with L-dopa. These patients have a type of **parkinsonism** (not true Parkinson's disease) that has turned their bodies into "statues" that have been "frozen" into a rigid position for many years. The L-dopa treatment brings the patients out of their total body triangle. Only nearby neurons that have **receptors** capable of attaching to this triangle shape can actually receive the chemical signal. If a neuron does not have a triangular receptor that this chemical can attach to, then that neuron does not get the signal and is not activated. A healthy brain works properly when all its neurons are able to receive the chemical signals intended for them. A neurologically healthy body is one in which these signals are passed, without a hitch, through the neurons in the brain, to the neurons in the spinal cord, through the spinal cord, and out to the proper neurons in the body (and back to the brain).

rigidity. For the first time in decades, the patients are normal—they can walk, talk, move, and react to the world in the same way as everyone else. Their "awakening" is amazing and heartwarming, but over time, the L-dopa stops working and their symptoms return. The movie is a celebration of life—revealing

This is a scene from the movie *Awakenings*, which is about how L-dopa helped people with a type of parkinsonism.

why everyone should appreciate the many good things in life. Yet it is also a story of how hard it often is to conquer a mysterious disease.

Different parts of the brain are involved in Parkinson's disease. Most of these structures are located deep inside the brain. Note that the substantia nigra is located at the top of the brain stem. The substantia nigra produces the neurotransmitter dopamine within the brain. Dopamine is an inhibiting neurotransmitter; that is, it is a chemical that signals "off" to a motor neuron (motor neurons are neurons that control body movement). Dopamine's opposite number, **acetylcholine**, is an "on," or motor-neuron-activating, neurotransmitter. In the healthy brain, there is a constant interaction and fine balance between acetylcholine and dopamine.

One of the most important brain structures involved in controlling movement is the corpus striatum, or simply the **striatum**, which is located deep within the brain. The striatum constantly receives signals that tell it about the body's position and movement. These signals come from other parts of the brain that continuously get information directly from specific parts of the body. For example, just getting up out of a chair requires an astoundingly complex series of many thousands of signals between various body parts and the brain. Specific areas of the brain, which receive impulses from nerves attached to muscles, communicate constantly with the striatum. The striatum monitors every movement to make sure a person does not fall over while he or she bends to rise, ensures that he or she places his or her feet in the proper position on the floor, and cues the correct muscles to flex or contract to get him or her out of his or her seat. During every minute change in her body that occurs as he or she completes this simple action, many thousands of signals carried by acetylcholine are analyzed by the striatum to make sure he or she is moving properly. The striatum is also in constant communication with the substantia nigra, which is releasing dopamine.

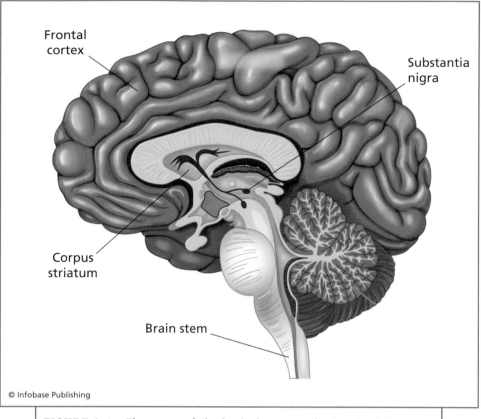

Frontal
cortex

Substantia
nigra

Corpus
striatum

Brain stem

© Infobase Publishing

FIGURE 3.4   The parts of the brain known to be involved in Parkinson's disease include the corpus striatum, the substantia nigra, and the brain stem.

To sum up, smooth, coordinated movement involves a delicate balance between acetylcholine and dopamine. Together, these neurotransmitters are used by specialized neurons in the brain to fine-tune the way the body moves.

THE PARKINSON BRAIN

If the substantia nigra is not working properly and not producing sufficient dopamine, the simple action of getting up out of a chair can become difficult. The release of acetyl-choline by some neurons could get the body moving, but there would be no inhibiting dopamine signal to control the motion. The striatum would not get the dopamine signal needed to limit the motion.

Dopamine is a very rare neurotransmitter that occurs in tiny amounts. In fact, only about 450,000 neurons in the substantia nigra produce dopamine—that is a tiny 0.0001% of all brain cells. Dopamine is stored in tiny sacs at the ends of substantia nigra neurons. When needed, the sacs release their dopamine into the synapse. The shape of the dopamine molecule allows it to attach to dopamine recep-tors on nearby neurons. Impulses pass from one neuron to another until they reach the striatum, which helps control body movement.

In the normal brain, dopamine molecules attach to the receptors on nearby neurons for only a split second. Then the receptors release the dopamine molecules back into the fluid that fills the synapse. From there, the dopamine mole-cules are pumped back into the substantia nigra cells where they were produced, and they remain in these neurons until they are needed again.

Unfortunately, there is a catch. Two enzymes in brain fluid lie in wait for dopamine molecules that have completed their mission and are ready to return to their home neuron. These two enzymes, **COMT** and **MAO-B**, attack dopamine

(opposite) **FIGURE 3.5**   In the normal brain (a), all the substantia nigra cells release dopamine into the synapse, and the dopamine attaches to receptors on nearby neurons. In the Parkinson's brain (b), the dotted lines represent substantia nigra cells that have died. Thus, the neurons near them do not receive dopamine. Only one functioning substantia nigra cell is shown that is capable of releasing dopamine to receptors on nearby neurons.

molecules and change them into a useless chemical that is eventually excreted from the body. It is estimated that 20% of dopamine molecules released by substantia nigra cells

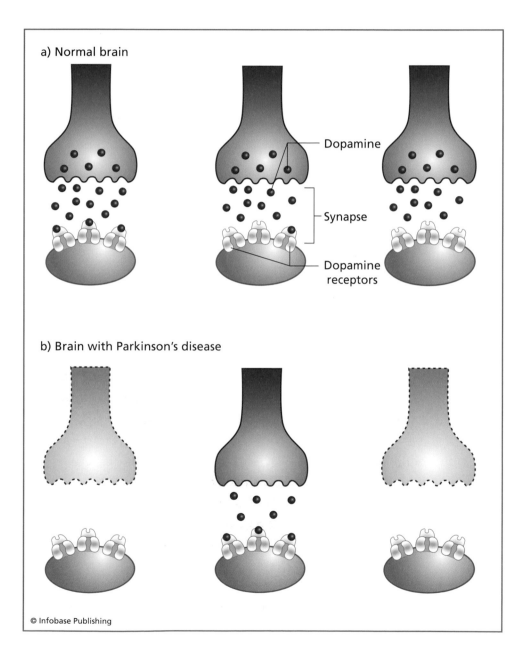

a) Normal brain

Dopamine

Synapse

Dopamine
receptors

b) Brain with Parkinson's disease

© Infobase Publishing

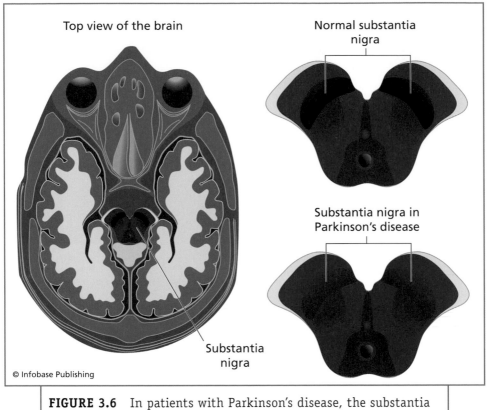

Top view of the brain

Normal substantia nigra

Substantia nigra in Parkinson's disease

Substantia nigra

© Infobase Publishing

FIGURE 3.6   In patients with Parkinson's disease, the substantia nigra begins to shrink as its cells die.

are destroyed in this way. This occurs in a normal brain. Little is known about why this seemingly senseless destruction occurs. Yet it makes the effects of Parkinson's disease that much more devastating.

In the brain of an individual with Parkinson's disease, more and more of the dopamine-producing neurons in the substantia nigra stop functioning and die. As the disease progresses, less and less dopamine is produced and transmitted to other neurons. Yet the same amount of acetylcholine continues to be present. With less of the inhibiting chemical available, body movement becomes increasingly uncontrolled.

As more substantia nigra cells die, those that remain alive increase their dopamine production to compensate for the lost dopamine. In some substantia nigra neurons, dopamine production increases fivefold. This increase in dopamine production may help temporarily stave off the worst effects of Parkinson's. However, as more cells die, eventually there is too little dopamine to control the body's motion. When only 20% of substantia nigra cells remain, the symptoms of Parkinson's disease appear. Dopamine is no longer available to control body movement. Without the needed chemical inhibition, muscles tend to move constantly and uncontrollably, causing tremors. Without the inhibiting neurotransmitter, joints and muscles become stiff, posture and balance deteriorate, and moving becomes difficult.

The obvious question is: What causes the cells in the substantia nigra to begin to die? No one knows for sure, but as Chapter 4 explores, medical science is investigating several key suspects.

4

WHAT CAUSES PARKINSON'S DISEASE?

Scientists know that the death of dopamine-producing cells in the substantia nigra causes Parkinson's disease. What researchers have yet to find out is what causes these cells to die. What medical researchers have found, though, is that any one of several unrelated conditions or events might affect the substantia nigra. There might not be one single cause of Parkinson's disease, but several. This chapter reviews what is known about the most significant and most likely causes of Parkinson's disease.

OVERACTIVE CELLS

Some researchers today are studying the role that cell chemicals and processes have on the substantia nigra's neurons. These researchers are trying to find out if **oxidative stress** causes Parkinson's. **Oxidation** is a chemical reaction that occurs in all normal body cells. A nonbiological example of oxidation is the formation of rust. When iron is in a moist environment, it combines chemically with the oxygen in the air to form a new substance called rust. This process is called oxidation because it involves one substance combining chemically with oxygen to form another substance. In the body, too much oxidation may harm cells. Researchers have noted that inside substantia nigra cells, dopamine is **metabolized** through an oxidation process. The researchers are testing the hypothesis that too much oxidation of dopamine may end up damaging the substantia nigra cells themselves. This is called oxidative stress.

As of now, there is no direct evidence that too much oxidation fatally damages substantia nigra cells. Researchers have also failed to determine what causes a cell to begin overoxidizing dopamine. Thus, although this hypothesis is interesting, there is not yet any evidence to show that oxidative stress is the cause of Parkinson's.

ORGANELLES AND ENZYMES

Scientists who study the brain cells of Parkinson's patients consistently find abnormalities in cell organelles called **mitochondria.** Mitochondria are tiny organelles that have an extremely important job: They burn fuel (which comes from food) to generate the energy the cell needs to function. The processes carried out by mitochondria are extremely complex, but they have been broken down into four basic parts, simply called complexes I, II, III, and IV. In people with Parkinson's, complex I processes do not work properly, because the mitochondria are not normal. These abnormal mitochondria are found in the neurons of the person's brain, as well as in muscle and blood cells. The reduced complex I function is, scientists have found, somehow related to Parkinson's disease. The scientists also found that coenzyme Q, an important part of mitochondria, also occurs at very low levels in people with Parkinson's.

There are ongoing clinical trials in which Parkinson's patients are being treated with high doses of coenzyme Q.

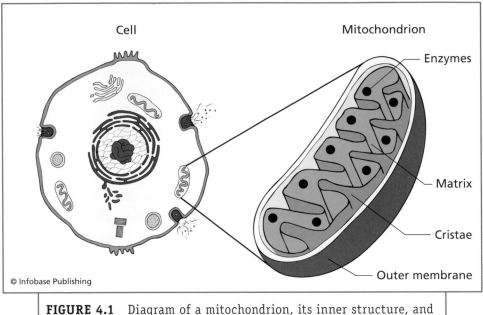

© Infobase Publishing

FIGURE 4.1   Diagram of a mitochondrion, its inner structure, and its placement in a cell

These trials seem to be having a positive effect on the patients' condition. However, exactly how and why mitochondrial complex I fails to function properly, and why coenzyme Q (among all the mitochondria's enzymes) seems to help, is still not understood.

ENVIRONMENTAL TOXINS

Researchers are also investigating the role of environmental factors in Parkinson's. Some environmental factors they are investigating are toxic substances—such as illegal drugs or **pesticides**—and physical brain injuries.

Stranger than Fiction

In 1977, a young man—let's call him X—decided to go into the illegal drug business. He set up a lab in his home in

Virginia. X found a medical journal that he thought contained a "recipe" for the prescription painkiller he wanted to make and sell illegally. X followed the drug recipe and took some of the chemical concoction he had made. In a very short time, he became extremely ill. Shortly thereafter, his body became so rigid he could not move. In his frozen, rigid state, he was transported to a nearby hospital.

The doctor on duty diagnosed X's symptoms as Parkinson's disease. X was treated for a while with anti-Parkinson's medication. X's symptoms improved for a short time, but soon his total body rigidity returned. He was then sent to a hospital associated with the U.S. National Institutes of Health (NIH) in Maryland. While treating X, the doctors followed his recipe to reproduce the drug he had made. What they found astonished them. X had mistakenly overheated his recipe, unwittingly making a poisonous chemical called MPTP (1-methyl-4-phenyl-1,2,3,6-tetrahydropyridine). Lab tests revealed that even tiny amounts of MPTP cause severe Parkinson's symptoms. The researchers also found that the MPTP left accumulations of another dangerous substance, MPP^+, in the brain.

Despite constant treatment, X died. His **autopsy** showed that all the cells in his substantia nigra were destroyed. Several years later, in 1982, a number of heroin addicts were admitted to hospitals in California with the same symptoms X had had. Tests revealed that the drugs they had bought on the street also contained MPTP.

After a few years of research, scientists determined why MPTP produced Parkinson's symptoms. It is not the MPTP itself that is harmful. Instead, the investigators found that when MPTP enters the body, it comes into contact with an enzyme called MAO-B (monoamine oxidase inhibitor, type B). The MAO-B enzyme breaks down the MPTP into the highly toxic MPP^+ (1-methyl-4-phenyl-hydroxypiperidine).

It is the MPP$^+$ that destroys the substantia nigra cells and causes the Parkinson's symptoms. Interestingly, MAO-B is the enzyme that also breaks down dopamine after it is released by substantia nigra neurons.

From this research, the scientists were able to create a drug—deprenyl—that inhibits or blocks the action of MAO-B, and thus prevents it from creating MPP$^+$. Though deprenyl (also called selegiline) was tested as a treatment for Parkinson's, it was found to have limited effectiveness. It seemed to relieve some symptoms, but only for a short period, after which they returned. The medical researchers were forced to conclude that once MPP$^+$ was created and began destroying cells, the damage was irreversible. However, the definite connection between MPP$^+$ and Parkinson's has opened a new avenue of research that might one day yield a successful treatment for the disease.

People at Risk

There are remarkable similarities between the condition produced by MPP$^+$ and true Parkinson's disease. The resemblance is so uncanny that many scientists speculate there may be natural substances that induce production of MPP$^+$ in the body.

There are certain human-made toxins—particularly specific pesticides—that contain chemicals related to MPP$^+$. In fact, researchers have learned that people who live and work in agricultural areas are on average seven times more likely to develop Parkinson's disease than people who live far from areas routinely sprayed with these pesticides.

Research has revealed that exposure to the pesticides rotenone and dieldrin can lead to classic Parkinson's symptoms, including rigidity and progressive loss of dopamine-producing cells. Rotenone was also correlated with the presence of Lewy bodies in the neurons of the substantia

MUHAMMAD ALI

Professional boxers are routinely battered in the head, which may lead to brain injury. Muhammad Ali, one of the greatest boxers of all time, may have been able to "float like a butterfly and sting like a bee," as he famously claimed, but his brilliant boxing

Muhammad Ali, seen here with actor Michael J. Fox, was one of the world's greatest prize fighters. Head injuries he received in the boxing ring may have caused the parkinsonism from which this great athlete now suffers.

skills could not save him from what most physicians call "pugilistic parkinsonism" (*pugilistic* refers to aggression, fighting, or violence). It often takes only a few good punches to the head to set the process in motion.

The brain is surrounded by a liquid in which it floats inside the skull. When a boxer is punched in the head, the brain crashes against the skull. This may cause brain damage. Repeat this insult often enough, and significant brain damage may result. If the brain damage includes those structures involved in dopamine production or reception, then parkinsonism may ensue.

Once Ali retired from fighting, he experienced ever-worsening symptoms, including tremors, muscle stiffness and rigidity, and loss of muscle control. There are some medical researchers who claim that trauma did not cause Ali's symptoms. Instead, they contend that Muhammad Ali has true Parkinson's disease that

(continues)

(continued)

was caused by something other than brain damage sustained in the boxing ring. They base their opinion on the fact that Ali responds well to drugs used to treat true Parkinson's disease. Whatever type of disease he has, it is heartbreaking to see this once vibrant and mighty champion suffering from such a physically debilitating disease.

nigra. Even long-term, low-level exposure to the now-banned but still environmentally persistent dieldrin often leads to Parkinson's in later life. People who are exposed to the pesticide paraquat have been found to have three times the normal risk for developing Parkinson's. This pesticide was shown to cause the buildup of a protein in the brain that is associated with Parkinson's (as discussed in Chapter 9). In fact, research has shown that early exposure to pesticides is associated with early development of Parkinson's disease.

Aluminum is another ubiquitous substance in the environment that has been closely linked with Parkinson's (as well as Alzheimer's disease). Abnormally high levels of aluminum have been found in the substantia nigra cells of Parkinson's patients.

Scientists have not ruled out an environmental cause of Parkinson's disease. Yet the question arises: Why do some people exposed to these substances develop true Parkinson's disease, while others who have the same exposure do not become ill?

Increasingly, researchers are seeking the cause of Parkinson's disease in the **genetic** makeup of individuals. Perhaps some people have **genes** that lead to mitochondrial abnormalities or make them particularly susceptible to Parkinson's disease after exposure to certain environmental poisons, while others do not have these genes. The research under way into possible genetic causes of Parkinson's disease is discussed in detail in Chapter 8.

Parkinsonism

The unfortunate X, whose homemade drugs caused his eventual death, may not have suffered from what physicians call true Parkinson's disease (even though his condition led to advances in the understanding of the disease). He may, in fact, have fallen victim to what doctors call parkinsonism—a condition that closely resembles true Parkinson's but may not be the actual disease.

Parkinsonism has many of the same symptoms as true Parkinson's, including tremor, rigidity, and loss of muscle control and balance. However, it may lack some of the telltale characteristics of the actual disease, such as the presence of Lewy bodies in the dead substantia nigra neurons.

There are several conditions or events that may lead to parkinsonism. Certain prescription drugs—including certain drugs used to treat psychiatric and digestive disorders as well as high blood pressure—may initiate the onset of parkinsonian symptoms because the drugs interfere with dopamine production in the brain. Fortunately, these symptoms disappear once the drug is withdrawn.

Head trauma is also known to sometimes produce parkinsonism. Accidents that involve damage to the brain may kill or damage some brain cells, including those of the substantia nigra, or they may reduce production of neurotransmitters or neuroreceptors to the point where parkinsonian symptoms appear. Some scientists believe that head trauma

produces true Parkinson's disease. They base their conclusion on the fact that the symptoms appear gradually and get
worse over time. If the injury did not cause true Parkinson's,
the brain damage and its symptoms would occur all at once,
rather than worsening over time.

5

SYMPTOMS AND THE DISEASE PROCESS

Sometimes, people may have to carry heavy objects or boxes for an extended period of time. When they are finally done, they may notice that their arms are shaking. Do they have Parkinson's disease? No. They have a touch of muscle strain. At other times, they may wake up and find that their hand or arm is numb or may be a bit shaky, and they wonder if they have Parkinson's. If the numbness or shakiness goes away in a few minutes, they do not. All that happened was that they slept in a position that put prolonged pressure on a nerve in their hand.

This chapter presents an overview of the symptoms of Parkinson's and the process of the disease over time. How Parkinson's is diagnosed is the subject of Chapter 6.

EARLY SYMPTOMS

In almost all cases, the initial symptoms of Parkinson's disease begin on only one side of the body. No one knows why this is the case, but it is characteristic of the disease. In fact, it may take years for symptoms to affect the other side of the body. Studies have shown that handedness is not related to which side of the body is first affected. For example, if a person is right-handed, there is no evidence

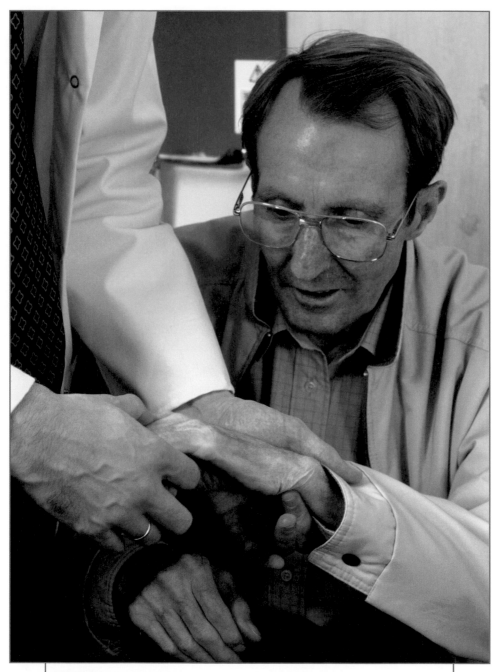

FIGURE 5.1 Doctors examine the hands of people who are diagnosed with Parkinson's disease to check for signs of muscle stiffness.

that initial symptoms will occur in the right hand or in the left hand.

Tremor

For most people, the first obvious symptom of Parkinson's disease is mild tremor, usually in the hand or fingers, when the limb is at rest. About 75% of people diagnosed with Parkinson's report this as their first noticeable symptom.[11] It is less common for initial tremors to occur in the feet, legs, jaw, or lips. Rarer still are tremors beginning in the head or neck. In most cases, these early tremors stop when the person goes to sleep. They also often stop when the person engages in voluntary (deliberate) movement.

Occasionally, people with the initial symptoms of Parkinson's report having the feeling of tremor inside the body. Internal tremor usually occurs in the limbs or torso. These internal tremors are not visible; they are just a feeling of inner trembling.

Rigidity

A common early symptom of Parkinson's is stiffness in the limbs. Parkinson's causes muscles to tighten up and remain contracted. For this reason, people with early Parkinson's may find that they have trouble moving. Their muscles no longer contract and relax in a smooth, coordinated way, so they experience muscle rigidity.

Muscle stiffness may reveal itself as toe curling, when the toes turn upward involuntarily. Sometimes, a person's feet seem to "freeze" and cannot move. This condition may result in a person's walking with a shuffling gait because he or she cannot lift and flex his or her feet normally.

Rigidity may take the form of what doctors call masked face, a condition in which rigidity of the face muscles makes a person unable to show spontaneous facial expressions. People with facial rigidity may appear to be distracted, staring, or even depressed. They may not blink their eyes as often as normal people do.

Because of muscle rigidity, Parkinson's sufferers may lose the ability to use their hands in a smooth and dexterous manner. They may feel clumsy and be unable to use a computer keyboard, fasten a button, or do other simple tasks that require fine muscle control. Often, they may find that their handwriting changes. Muscle stiffness often leads to what is called **micrographia**, a gradual shrinking of a person's handwriting.

Aches and Pains

Some people with initial symptoms of Parkinson's may experience a variety of aches and pains caused by muscle stiffness and contraction. Most often, aches occur in the neck, shoulders, arms, legs, or lower back. As with tremor, most pains begin on only one side of the body.

Some people report feelings of numbness, tingling, burning, coldness, or aching in their legs, arms, back, or abdomen. These pains come and go, but they are disturbing and uncomfortable when they do occur.

A limited number of new Parkinson's patients may find that they wake up with foot cramps. These cramps cause the toes to curl downward or the big toe to bend up while the other toes curl down. Rarely is the hand similarly affected. Foot cramps can be quite common among healthy people, so people should not be alarmed and think they have Parkinson's if they occasionally experience a foot or toe cramp if this is their only symptom.

Posture

A stooped posture is sometimes an early sign of Parkinson's disease. The stoop is produced by the contraction of the muscles. However, a stoop may simply be a sign of aging, so by itself it is not a definite sign of Parkinson's.

RARE SYMPTOMS OF PARKINSON'S

Some symptoms are very rare. The following symptoms of Parkinson's occur in less than 50% of patients.

- ◆ **Dementia**: disorientation, confusion, memory loss
- ◆ Chewing and swallowing problems: muscles in the mouth and throat are affected
- ◆ Slurred speech
- ◆ Frozen shoulder: intense rigidity "freezes" the shoulder and prevents movement

PROGRESSIVE SYMPTOMS OF PARKINSON'S DISEASE

As time passes, the symptoms of Parkinson's disease become worse. Initial symptoms become more intense, and new symptoms often arise.

Voice

People suffering from Parkinson's often experience a softening, or loss of power, in their voice. They find that they can no longer speak loudly, or they have to struggle to maintain their voice's volume. They must force themselves to make their voice audible. This condition may make it difficult for Parkinson's patients to talk on the telephone (though a voice amplifier often helps). They may also have difficulty at work if they have to speak to a group in meetings or other workplace gatherings.

Walking and Moving

Normally, the arms move as a person walks. In the normal motion, the arms easily swing back and forth as a person walks. People with Parkinson's do not swing their arms when they walk. Sometimes, this symptom appears early, when the arm on the affected side of the body remains rigid at the person's side when walking. This symptom gets progressively worse over time. Eventually, both arms remain rigid when a person walks.

When rigidity increases in one leg, Parkinson's patients move as if they are dragging the rigid leg behind them. They may appear to walk with a limp. As time passes, they often find that they have increasing difficulty getting up out of a low, soft chair or getting in and out of a car.

Balance

Though unsteadiness may be an early symptom of Parkinson's, real lack of balance usually occurs later in the illness. There are many complex reflexes involved in simply keeping a person moving upright. In Parkinson's, these reflexes involved with balance deteriorate.

As a person's balance gets worse, there is a real danger of falling and injury. People with Parkinson's may have trouble turning around quickly or balancing on one foot (as when standing and pulling on a boot). Walking on an uneven surface makes the balance problem worse. Eventually, Parkinson's sufferers may be so affected that they fall without any noticeable reason.

To make up for poor balance and lack of muscle coordination, Parkinson's patients may tend to walk very fast (the running walk described by Dr. James Parkinson) as a way to help them keep their balance.

In severe cases, a person may suddenly "freeze" and be unable to move at all. Sometimes, such patients fall over if the freezing occurs while they were in rapid motion. This symptom is generally very distressing to Parkinson's patients.

PSYCHOLOGICAL PROBLEMS

Most of the psychological problems associated with Parkinson's are related to the shock of its diagnosis and the difficulty of living with its symptoms. Most people who experience depression when they are first diagnosed recover in a short time. However, some people experience

A FRIEND IN NEED

Everyone knows that seeing-eye dogs are trained to help the blind get around. Yet most people do not know that dogs are also trained to help people with Parkinson's disease. Parkinson's helper dogs are trained to help Parkinson's patients walk and keep their balance. For example, when the dog senses that her owner is off-balance, the dog positions herself to help the person regain balance. Often, the dog is trained to place her paw on the patient's foot to stop the patient's motion and provide time for balance to be restored. Parkinson's helper dogs have been trained to help lift a person who has fallen, help a patient who freezes to

Dogs can be trained to help people with Parkinson's disease. In the photograph above, the man with the dog has Parkinson's disease. The helping dog places its paw on the man's foot to help him regain his balance.

move again, flip light switches, open doors, pick up objects that have fallen on the floor, and even push wheelchairs. For many Parkinson's patients, having a helper dog allows them to live a safer and more independent life.

severe, long-term depression, and they must be treated with medication for this condition.

More rarely, people with Parkinson's report feeling very anxious and agitated. Both are usually reactions to the diagnosis and living with the disease. Anxiety, and its more

IS PERSONALITY CONNECTED TO PARKINSON'S?

Some people have wondered if there is a relationship between the type of personality a person has and his or her likelihood of getting Parkinson's disease. Even some medical professionals have noted that there appear to be some personality character-istics that seem to be related to Parkinson's. These include being very strict, or "straight laced," and avoiding the use of alcohol or tobacco.

Of course, not all people who have these traits develop Par-kinson's, and many people who do not have these traits do get the disease. However, researchers have used brain imaging technology, primarily positron emission tomography (PET) and single photon emission computed tomography (SPECT) scans, to reveal that at least some of these traits may arise from Parkin-son's disease itself years before it is diagnosed. Studies show that changes occur in the brains of those who develop Parkin-son's five years or more before the first symptoms appear. These changes in the brain may account for the personality traits described above. Some scientists who are working on develop-ing drugs to treat Parkinson's are concentrating on identifying people with these preclinical (before symptoms) signs of the disease so they can start treatment before the disease symp-toms arise. Perhaps they will develop a drug that prevents the onset of Parkinson's symptoms.

severe form—panic attacks—can be successfully treated with drugs. Apathy, or loss of interest and motivation in life, is less common and is almost always a response to the difficulty of living with Parkinson's. Although this condition is harder to treat with medications, mental-health counseling may be beneficial.

SUMMARY: THE STAGES OF PARKINSON'S

As with most progressive disorders, doctors divide Parkinson's disease into different stages, each defined by its symptoms. Stage I is the earliest, and Stage V is the most advanced form of the illness.

Stage I
- Early symptoms appear on only one side of the body.
- Symptoms are not disabling.
- Tremors occur in one limb.

Stage II
- Symptoms develop on both sides of the body.
- Problems with walking and posture develop.
- Symptoms cause some disability.

Stage III
- Body movement slows down considerably.
- Balance is noticeably impaired.
- Symptoms cause major problems with normal functioning.

Stage IV
- Symptoms become severe.
- Walking becomes very difficult.

◆ Rigidity and slowness of motion become worse.
◆ Help is needed to conduct everyday activities.

Stage V

◆ Patient becomes bedridden, needs a wheelchair and/or constant care.

Not all Parkinson's sufferers progress to Stages IV or V. New treatments are being developed that arrest the disease's symptoms before they become this debilitating.[12]

6

DIAGNOSIS OF PARKINSON'S DISEASE

Parkinson's disease is just one of many conditions that may have the same or very similar symptoms. Some of these conditions are referred to as parkinsonism—diseases that are like Parkinson's disease but are not true Parkinson's. For this reason, it is sometimes extremely difficult for doctors to diagnose Parkinson's disease. It often takes many visits, ongoing observation, and several medical tests before a doctor can be sure that Parkinson's disease is the correct diagnosis.

INITIAL COMPLAINT

Most often, people visit their family doctor, or general practitioner, once they notice that they have a resting hand tremor that does not go away. The family doctor likely knows the patient's medical history. Perhaps the doctor knows that a medication the patient is taking may cause tremors as a side effect. If that is the case, the family doctor may tell the patient to stop using the medication or to use a different medication that does not have tremors as a side effect. After about two weeks without the medication, the patient visits the doctor again. If the tremor is gone, then it was certainly the medication that caused the tremor. The patient does not have Parkinson's disease.

If the patient stops the medication but still has resting hand tremors, then it is clear that the medication did not cause the tremor. In this case, it is likely that the family doctor will refer the patient to a specialist—a neurologist who specializes in Parkinson's disease.

There are other conditions the general practitioner might try to diagnose before he or she concludes the patient likely has Parkinson's disease. For example, manganese is a metal

THE "RULING OUT" RULE

Doctors often reach an accurate diagnosis by first ruling out diseases or conditions that they think are *not* what their patient is suffering from. For example, if a patient with the early symptoms of Parkinson's shows up at a neurologist's office, one of the first things the doctor may do is have the patient walk around a lot. If the patient falls down easily or shows extreme imbalance at this early stage, then the physician can be fairly certain that the person does not have true Parkinson's disease. Falling down and extreme imbalance are not among the initial symptoms of Parkinson's disease. Also, if the patient experienced symptoms suddenly—that is, if they did not come on gradually—then, again, the doctor can rule out true Parkinson's. Other signs that allow a doctor to rule out Parkinson's are low blood pressure leading to fainting, very rapid physical deterioration, and medications the patient may be taking. In short, physicians often try to rule out what a condition is *not* before they zero in on what it *is*. This approach is especially useful for hard-to-diagnose conditions such as Parkinson's disease.

that some people might be exposed to at their place of work. If too much manganese gets into the body, it can cause parkinsonian symptoms. Diseases of the Lewy bodies may cause parkinsonian symptoms, as may certain types of small strokes. In fact, there are many (usually rare) conditions that present parkinsonian symptoms. In most cases, diseases or conditions that mimic Parkinson's involve the brain and other parts of the nervous system, so a family doctor will usually refer the patient to a neurologist.

THE NEUROLOGIST TAKES CHARGE

One of the first and most important things a neurologist will do is take a complete personal and family medical history from the patient, including information about medications, possible exposure to toxic substances, and details about when and how the symptoms first appeared. While taking the history, the doctor will take care to observe if the patient's hands are trembling in his or her lap, if he or she has a "masked face," if his or her voice is unusually soft, and other easily observed signs of disease. The neurologist will then often question the patient to find out if he or she has experienced some of the symptoms of Parkinson's disease. During this first conversation, the neurologist may also ask factual questions to determine if the patient has a type of dementia, such as Alzheimer's disease, instead of Parkinson's disease.

The physician will then have the patient perform simple tasks to determine which symptoms are visible. For example, the doctor will ask the patient to rise from the chair to see if that action is difficult; to walk a short distance so the doctor can observe signs of rigidity, lack of arm movement, and stooped posture; to sign his or her name on a piece of paper to note signs of micrographia; to stand on one foot to determine how good his or her balance is; and to put together the pieces in a fairly simple puzzle to determine coordination. The neurologist will also examine the patient's eyes to check for eye-muscle rigidity and test the patient's reflexes.

Testing

There is no single diagnostic test that can confirm that a person definitely has Parkinson's disease. What neurological tests can do, however, is rule out conditions that are *not* true Parkinson's. For example, simple blood tests can point to other conditions that mimic Parkinson's. Brain scans, such

DIAGNOSTIC SCANS

Modern scan techniques allow physicians to view organs inside the body without resorting to surgery, which, in the past, was the only option. Three of these techniques are the CT, MRI, and PET scans.

Computerized tomography, known as a CT or CAT scan, can produce images of the internal structure of the brain or other organs. In a CT scan, a machine beams X-rays into the body from many different angles. The image taken from each angle is called a slice. Each slice shows one cross section of the organ being imaged. When the test is done, all the slices are sent to a computer, which puts them together to form a single, three-dimensional image. CT scans are especially useful for detecting anatomical abnormalities in an organ.

Magnetic resonance imaging (MRI) is done in a doughnut-shaped machine that holds an enormous magnet. The patient is placed in the middle of the large magnetic field produced by the magnet. The tissue being imaged absorbs radio waves emitted by the machine. When the radio waves are turned off, the as CT (computerized tomography) and MRI (magnetic resonance imaging) scans, help the neurologist rule out other causes for the symptoms, such as brain tumors, strokes, or other brain abnormalities. In people who have the early symptoms of true Parkinson's, however, CT and MRI scans appear normal because the changes occurring in the brain take place on a chemical and molecular level that is impossible to capture with these scans.

A PET (positron emission tomography) scan, which is very expensive, can be used to detect tiny changes in

hydrogen atoms gradually return to their original alignment, and the tissue releases the energy it has absorbed. This release of energy creates an image on a computer monitor.

Before a patient receives a positron emission tomography (PET) scan, he or she gets an injection of a weakly radioactive, sugary substance, which circulates throughout the body. All the body's cells absorb this sugary substance. However, the radioactive part of the substance begins to break down immediately, giving off gamma rays (or atomic particles called positrons). A PET scanner can "see" the particles being given off by each type of body cell. The rays appear as bright areas on a computer monitor. When one type of tissue is damaged, it absorbs less of the radioactive substance and gives off fewer rays. Diseased tissue appears less bright, or even totally dark, on the PET scan computer screen. By pinpointing the exact part of the brain that has damaged or diseased tissue, PET scans enable doctors to make diagnoses that were previously impossible.

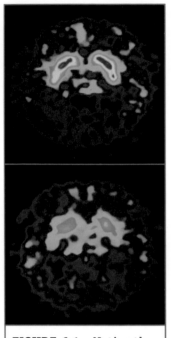

FIGURE 6.1 Notice the difference in these PET scans of a normal brain (a) and a Parkinson's brain (b). The lack of color seen in the central brain of the person with Parkinson's disease indicates the degeneration of the substantia nigra.

the brain, even changes in the brain's chemistry. In a PET scan, a radioactive substance injected into the patient becomes concentrated in the substantia nigra area of the brain. The PET scanner then measures the activity of dopamine neurons in the area. **Figure 6.1** shows the dramatic changes that occur in the brain of a person who has Parkinson's disease. A PET scan is most useful as Parkinson's disease progresses and is usually less revealing in very early Parkinson's disease.

In 1998, a researcher at Harvard University developed a new and exciting method, called single photon emission computed tomography (SPECT), that has the potential for accurate early diagnosis and ongoing monitoring of the disease's progression. In a SPECT scan, altropane, a chemical that specifically binds to dopamine transporters in the cells of the substantia nigra, is injected into the body. Cells that absorb altropane are visualized as bright areas in a SPECT scan. Because altropane binds to single neurons, the new technique is capable of producing an image of moderate, and sometimes even early, Parkinson's disease. This new test may permit positive diagnosis of Parkinson's at earlier stages, thus improving the chances that quick and aggressive treatment may slow down the disease process. Repeated SPECT scans also enable physicians to monitor the progression of the disease and adjust the patient's treatment accordingly.

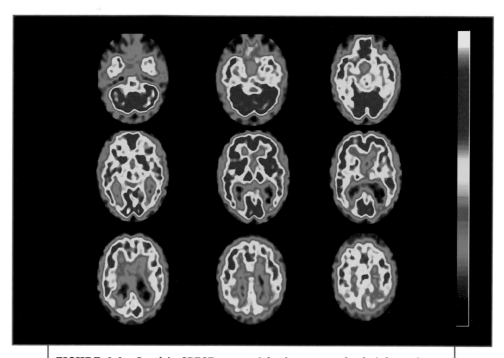

FIGURE 6.2 In this SPECT scan with altropane, the bright red areas are the substantia nigra—dopamine-producing cells—in the brain. As Parkinson's progresses, these areas become darker and smaller.

If the patient has all or most of the characteristic symptoms of Parkinson's disease, and if as many other conditions as possible are ruled out by testing, then the neurologist may make a tentative diagnosis of Parkinson's disease. The physician most likely will then prescribe a medication used to treat Parkinson's disease. The neurologist will want to see the patient every week or so for the next few months to determine if the medications are effective at reducing or eliminating the symptoms. If they are, then the neurologist can make a diagnosis of Parkinson's disease with a high degree of confidence, because other conditions that mimic Parkinson's do not respond to these medications. If the medications do not relieve the patient's symptoms, then the doctor knows that there is a high probability that the patient does not have true Parkinson's disease, and further testing is required to make a correct diagnosis.

7

TREATMENT OF PARKINSON'S DISEASE

Parkinson's is a progressive disease, so treatment often depends on the disease stage at which treatment begins. Several medications are quite effective in most cases. Other therapies are used to treat Parkinson's when medication does not produce the desired relief or becomes ineffective at controlling symptoms. In most cases, over time, treatment of the disease must be adjusted based on the progression of the symptoms. To date, all treatments for Parkinson's disease are intended only to treat its symptoms. As yet, there is no cure for Parkinson's disease.

Parkinson's symptoms may vary widely from patient to patient. For this reason, doctors use various approaches to treatment. In this chapter, the most typical Parkinson's treatments are covered.

ANTICHOLINERGIC DRUGS

If a person who is initially diagnosed with Parkinson's disease has mild resting tremor as the major or only symptom, the neurologist may begin treatment by prescribing an **anticholinergic** drug. Anticholinergic drugs act on the acetylcholine in the brain. (Remember that acetylcholine is the "on" neurotransmitter for motor function.) Anticholinergic drugs restore the balance between acetylcholine and dopamine by toning down or partially blocking the action of acetylcholine. Anticholinergic drugs can be very effective at reducing resting tremor.

Anticholinergic drugs may have many unpleasant side effects. These include dry mouth and eyes, blurred vision, reduced urination and perspiration (which hinders the body's ability to regulate its temperature), severe muscle cramps, and sometimes even hallucinations. Because of these many side effects, many neurologists today avoid prescribing anticholinergic drugs to treat resting tremor.

LEVODOPA

Levodopa is the brain chemical that is created during the process that leads to the production of dopamine. Levodopa is therefore a precursor from which dopamine is made.

After researchers discovered that Parkinson's disease involves a severe reduction in the amount of dopamine in the brain, they tried to treat the disease with doses of dopamine. Unfortunately, no matter how dopamine was given—by mouth or by injection—it seemed to have no effect on Parkinson's symptoms. It soon became clear that dopamine was ineffective because it could not cross the **blood-brain barrier**, a kind of selective roadblock in the brain composed of cells and small blood vessels. The blood-brain barrier protects the brain by keeping unwanted and potentially dangerous substances from entering the brain directly through the bloodstream. Once they realized that dopamine would not work, researchers began testing levodopa. They found that it could cross the blood-brain barrier—but only if it was given orally.

The Early Years of Levodopa

Levodopa, or L-dopa, began to be used to treat Parkinson's patients in the 1960s. The results were dramatic. After getting large doses of L-dopa, even the most severe symptoms seemed to melt away. People who had been confined to wheelchairs were able to play baseball and other sports. L-dopa seemed like a miracle cure.

As sometimes happens, what at first appeared to be a miracle cure soon revealed a darker side. Doctors soon discovered that patients had to receive enormous doses of L-dopa because a good deal of the drug's action took place not in the brain but in the gastrointestinal (GI) tract, which includes the stomach and intestines. It seems that a GI enzyme that helps create dopamine from levodopa was acting on the L-dopa while the drug was still in the GI tract, before it reached the brain. This was not only counterproductive, it also tended to cause nausea and vomiting in patients. Eventually, researchers isolated a chemical that inhibits the action of the GI enzyme in question. When patients received L-dopa combined with this inhibiting chemical, called carbidopa, they experienced little or no nausea and could get the same symptom relief with a smaller amount of the combination drug.

L-dopa therapy still had drawbacks. L-dopa activates dopamine production in the cells that produce dopamine—neurons of the substantia nigra. Yet as Parkinson's disease progresses, these cells die off, and there are fewer and fewer of them left. Medical researchers realized that they had to do something to overcome the flaw in the drug—its dependence on healthy substantia nigra cells. Finally, researchers developed a synthetic (human-made) drug that stimulates dopamine-sensitive receptor sites on neurons. The new medication, called a dopamine receptor agonist (an agonist is a chemical that attaches to cell receptors because it mimics the action of a neurotransmitter), imitates the way dopamine acts on dopamine receptors. In other words, the new synthetic drug disguised itself as "real" dopamine and tricked neuron receptors into acting as if it was dopamine. The new drug stimulates the transmission of dopamine-controlled nerve signals and, thus, helps relieve the symptoms of Parkinson's.

Since the development of this new type of L-dopa combination drug, other improvements have been added to the treatment regimen. Researchers have developed chemicals that inhibit other enzymes that interfere with dopamine production from levodopa. These drugs are called COMT inhibitors. (COMT is another enzyme that breaks down dopamine.) They have also developed MAO-inhibitors that help prevent MAO-B from destroying dopamine, thus making more dopamine available to neurons.

Levodopa Treatment Today

Many Parkinson's patients begin their treatment with a combination drug that is made up of levodopa and carbidopa. The L-dopa acts to produce dopamine, and the carbidopa works to inhibit the GI enzyme that destroys dopamine before it can reach the brain. This medication—called L-dopa for simplicity—comes in a variety of forms. Immediate-release L-dopa delivers its dose of symptom-relieving chemicals all at once. Controlled-release, or sustained-release, L-dopa is released in the body slowly, over time. Which type is best, and the best dosage, is determined by the neurologist and the patient based on how well each treatment works to relieve symptoms. In other words, drug therapy must be tailored for each individual patient.

One of the most common side effects of this L-dopa treatment is involuntary movement, called **dyskinesia**. Though dyskinesia is rare in the early years of L-dopa therapy, the longer a person takes L-dopa, the more likely it is that dyskinesia will develop. Dyskinesia is a dance-like, flowing movement of the arms, legs, or body that the person taking

L-dopa cannot control. The L-dopa controls tremors and rigidity but often causes this uncontrollable flowing motion. Because dyskinesia is not painful, many Parkinson's patients do not limit their L-dopa therapy to get rid of it. However, if the dyskinesia becomes disabling, different types of treatment may be required.

Levodopa Supplements

Some Parkinson's patients try to postpone beginning L-dopa treatment for as long as possible in the belief that, over time, L-dopa becomes less and less effective or its side effects (dyskinesia) become disturbingly worse. However, L-dopa does not lose its effectiveness over time. L-dopa seems to work less well because the brain is continually losing the dopamine-producing cells that L-dopa acts on.

Sometimes, the neurologist and the patient may decide to begin treatment not with L-dopa, but with a drug called selegiline. Selegiline is an MAO inhibitor. Taking this drug may increase the amount of dopamine in the brain because it helps prevent MAO from breaking down dopamine molecules in the synapse fluid. Further, selegiline blocks the toxicity of MPTP, which leads to parkinsonism and Parkinson's-like symptoms. There is still an ongoing medical debate—and continued research—about how effective selegiline is in either slowing the progression of Parkinson's disease or in alleviating its symptoms.

As Parkinson's disease progresses, different types of L-dopa, or L-dopa plus other medications, may be recommended. For example, a patient may begin drug treatment on the typical levodopa/carbidopa medication. As the patient's substantia nigra cells continue to die, a dopamine-receptor agonist drug may be added to the regimen. Or the neurologist may add a COMT- or MAO-inhibitor drug to the medications the patient must take. During late-stage Parkinson's, a patient may be taking all of the above medications. Generally, people with Parkinson's disease take some combination of medications throughout their life.

UNCONVENTIONAL TREATMENTS

As discussed in a previous chapter, MAO (monoamine oxidase) breaks down dopamine through a process of oxidation. For this reason, some patients and doctors have been exploring the use of natural antioxidants (not MAO-inhibitor drugs) in the treatment of Parkinson's.

Antioxidants

The most common natural antioxidants are vitamins—particularly vitamin C, vitamin E, vitamin D, and beta-carotene (a form of vitamin A). There have been few clinical trials conducted on the usefulness of these vitamins in slowing the progression of Parkinson's disease. One relatively small study that looked at whether high doses of vitamin E slowed the progression of Parkinson's yielded disappointing results. No positive effect was found.[13] However, larger studies on this and the other antioxidant vitamins may yield more promising results.

Coenzyme Q

Coenzyme Q occurs in cell mitochondria, cell organelles that do not function properly in patients with Parkinson's disease. A 2004 study showed that three high doses of coenzyme Q daily did have small but noticeable positive effects on the progression of the disease.[14] Though the researchers were happy with the positive results—however small—they remain skeptical about coenzyme Q's long-term effectiveness in halting the progression of Parkinson's. Research into coenzyme Q is ongoing, but it is still too early to state with any certainty whether coenzyme Q will become a useful weapon in the arsenal of drugs used to fight Parkinson's disease.

Coenzyme Q is not a prescription medication. It is sold over the counter at drug and health-food stores. Though it is expensive—especially when taken in very high doses—the research done so far seems to indicate that it has no noted side effects or adverse health effects (at least as determined by the 16-month study cited above). Neurologists caution against relying on the as yet unproven usefulness of coenzyme Q to slow down Parkinson's disease. They also point out that it does not seem to relieve the disease's symptoms.

Diet

Doctors have found that in some people, eating protein-rich foods interferes with the beneficial effects of Parkinson's

FULL OF BEANS

Medical researchers in Australia recently found that whole (with the pod) broad beans, or fava beans, contain a natural form of levodopa. Their research showed that 3.5 ounces (100 grams) of fava beans contain about 250 milligrams of levodopa. Parkinson's patients normally take between 300 and 2,500 mg of levodopa each day, so some patients would have to eat a lot of broad beans to get the required amount of levodopa. Still, the discovery of a natural form of this brain chemical may lead to development of a newer, more effective drug. Some patients may be able to limit their intake of medications and use diet to help control their disease. The whole beans were found to maintain their full level of levodopa after they were boiled, frozen, and even canned.

medications. For this reason, they recommend a "protein redistribution diet," in which patients eat low-protein foods in the morning and during the day—when the positive effects of medication are most important—and reserve their intake of protein-rich foods for the dinner hour. Of course, patients should still consume the amount of protein needed by the body. This diet just rearranges when the protein is eaten to maximize the benefits of the Parkinson's drugs. Neurologists often refer their Parkinson's patients to nutritionists, who help patients plan the best way and time to get the all protein they need.

Surgery

It often happens that Parkinson's symptoms (or drug side effects) become so disabling that patients seek other ways to control them. Surgery may be the treatment of choice for these patients. Brain surgery is a risky business, and it is not a cure for Parkinson's. Rather, it is a method for improving a patient's quality of life.

Surgery was first used to treat advanced Parkinson's in the 1930s, before levodopa treatment was developed. Surgeons targeted the cells in the parts of the brain that had become hyperactive due to the lack of dopamine. By destroying cells in the hyperactive parts of the brain, surgeons sought to re-create the natural balance that dopamine had once maintained. The earliest attempts to treat Parkinson's with surgery had mixed results. It was primarily lack of technology, not poor surgical skill, that led to poor outcomes. Because brain imaging was inadequate or nonexistent, too often important, nontargeted areas of the brain were destroyed along with the targeted regions. This sometimes left patients with brain damage and a new set of problems.

Parkinson's surgery became safer and more widely used in the 1960s. Experience taught neurosurgeons that two

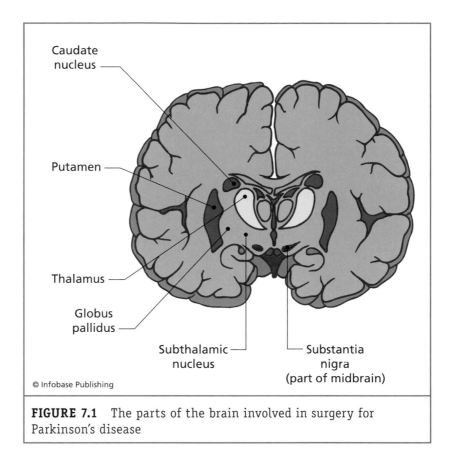

Caudate
nucleus

Putamen

Thalamus

Globus
pallidus

Subthalamic
nucleus

Substantia
nigra
(part of midbrain)

© Infobase Publishing

FIGURE 7.1   The parts of the brain involved in surgery for
Parkinson's disease

specific areas of the brain—the thalamus and the globus
pallidus—were the best targets for Parkinson's surgery. The
thalamus is a part of the brain that is central to the complex process of relaying nerve signals—especially those
involved in motor (muscle/movement) control—to and from
the brain and the body. The globus pallidus is also involved
in relaying these signals. In the 1960s, neurosurgeons performed thalamotomy (destruction of selected cells in the
thalamus) and pallidotomy (destruction of selected cells in
the globus pallidus) to provide relief from tremors and other
distressing Parkinson's symptoms. Still, because of the risk
that other parts of the brain might be injured, surgery was

generally reserved for only the most advanced cases of the disease.

With the development of L-dopa and other drugs in the 1960s, surgery lost favor as a treatment for Parkinson's. L-dopa and the drugs used in combination with it were highly effective, and the risk of brain damage during surgery seemed neither sensible nor desirable. Although thalamotomy has been completely abandoned in the United States (it is still sometimes performed in Japan and a few other nations), the 1990s saw an upswing in pallidotomies. Highly sophisticated imaging and surgical techniques made pallidotomy more effective and far less risky than it had once been. Today, pallidotomy may provide patients with relief, not from the symptoms of Parkinson's disease but from a side effect of Parkinson's medications—dyskinesia.

Deep-brain Stimulation

Perhaps the most common Parkinson's surgery done today is called deep-brain stimulation. This technique developed from the understanding that electrically stimulating brain cells could control or adjust their action. For example, high-frequency electrical stimulation turns the neurons in the brain off, or reduces their activity. When the electrical stimulation stops, the neurons are turned on again and begin their normal activity. Deep-brain stimulation is an outgrowth, or advancement, of the previously described brain surgery. Instead of destroying the brain cells, deep-brain stimulation turns them on and off temporarily, so brain cells are not destroyed. Deep-brain stimulation is used largely on neurons in the thalamus.

In deep-brain stimulation surgery, an electrode is carefully inserted into the thalamus. One end of the electrode is placed deep inside the brain, in contact with the target thalamus neurons. The other end of the electrode emerges from the brain and skull, extending to just beneath the scalp. The surgeon attaches a wire to this end of the electrode and runs it under the skin, all the way from the scalp to an area below the collarbone. There, the wire is connected to an electrical stimulation box that is implanted beneath the skin of the chest wall. (The stimulation box is similar to a pacemaker that someone with a heart condition may have implanted in the chest.) Thus, there is a complete electrical connection running from the stimulation box in the chest to the end of the electrode deep inside the brain.

The stimulation box contains a computer chip that can be programmed from the outside by the neurologist or neurosurgeon. The patient is able to control the stimulation box as well. The patient is given a magnet that he or she can pass over the box to change the strength, or frequency, of the electrical signal it gives off. Thus, if a Parkinson's patient is experiencing severe tremors, he or she can use the magnet to increase the frequency of the electrical signal given off by the box. The high-frequency signal travels from the box, through the wire, and to the electrode that is embedded in the deep brain. A high-frequency electrical signal reduces activity in the neurons in the vicinity of the deep-brain electrode. This helps stop or limit the tremors. When the tremors have passed, the patient can use the magnet to reduce the frequency of the electrical signal coming from the box, and the neurons are reactivated. In this way, the patient can control the stimulation box based on how he or she is feeling at the moment.

A third, newer site for electrode implantation—the subthalamic nucleus—is being used with notable success. The subthalamic nucleus is a region of the brain that stimulates the globus pallidus. Deep-brain stimulation of the subthalamic nucleus seems to have a better outcome in relieving the rigidity and tremors of Parkinson's disease, as well as dyskinesia, than other types of surgery. Long-term studies have shown that the beneficial effects of this type of surgery seem to last longer than other surgeries, and the patient is able to take a far lower dose of L-dopa and other medications after surgery.[15] However, this surgery poses its own risks. For example, deep stimulation of the subthalamic nucleus is accomplished via two electrodes, one from each side of the brain. This requires two surgeries, which doubles the surgical risk.

Like earlier types of brain surgery for Parkinson's, deep-brain stimulation is considered only when symptoms are severe. Brain surgery is far too risky to undergo unless it is absolutely essential. Even in the hands of the most skilled neurosurgeon, brain surgery still poses risks such as stroke, brain hemorrhage (bleeding), vision loss, and possibly paralysis. Infection and mechanical failure are also dangers, though the hardware used in the surgery is fairly easy to repair—except for the deep-brain electrode. Other factors make surgery a less attractive option for some patients, including those with dementia, extreme old age, and other serious medical problems (kidney or liver disease, for example). Deep-brain stimulation is mainly recommended only in cases of severe tremor, severe drug-induced dyskinesia, and nonresponse to medication. Again, it is important to remember that even this most advanced form of surgery is not a cure for Parkinson's disease. It is a new and effective (though not risk-free) means of treating the disease's symptoms.

Will medical science one day find a cure for Parkinson's disease? There are some new and exciting avenues of research currently under way that will be discussed in the last chapter of this book.

8

LOOKING FOR
A GENETIC CAUSE

In 1990, the U.S. government decided to spend as much money as it took to finance an all-out effort to unlock the secrets of the human **genome**. A genome is the complete genetic material—the complete set of genes—of an organism. Genes are the basic physical and functional units of **heredity**, which are passed from parents to offspring.

By the time Human Genome Project scientists announced that they had a "first draft" of the human genome, the federal government had shelled out more than $3 billion on the project. A final draft of the human genome was presented in 2006.

One major goal of the Human Genome Project—aside from identifying genes and their function—is to pinpoint genes that cause disease or make a person susceptible to disease. Many diseases, including Parkinson's, have been linked to faulty genes. The next section will review what genes are, how they work, and how they relate to human characteristics and physical functions.

GENE BASICS

Organisms are made up of cells, and cells carry out complex functions that keep organisms alive. Cells contain a substance called **deoxyribonucleic acid (DNA)** that carries genetic information. As the Nobel Prize–winning scientists James Watson and Francis Crick discovered in 1953, DNA consists of two strands that are bonded together and coiled to form a double helix. This can be visualized as a coiled or twisted ladder. Each strand of DNA is composed of a chain of repeating units called **nucleotides**. A nucleotide consists of a sugar (called deoxyribose), a phosphate group, and a nitrogen-containing base. The sides of the DNA ladder are made up of the sugar and phosphate groups. The rungs of the ladder are made up of pairs of bases bonded together. In DNA, there are four types of bases, and, therefore, four types of nucleotides. The bases are adenine (A), cytosine (C), guanine (G), and thymine (T).

The bonding between the bases, which holds the two strands of DNA together, is highly specific: A pairs only with T, and C pairs only with G. Therefore, wherever there is an A on one side of the ladder, a T on the other side completes the rung. Wherever there is a C on one strand, there is a G on the other. A specific sequence of nucleotides makes up a gene.

The human genome contains about 3 billion base pairs of nucleotides that are distributed among the approximately 30,000 genes that make up human DNA. DNA and associated proteins form structures called **chromosomes** that are found in the cell nucleus (in most organisms). Each human chromosome has its own set of genes that control, or help control, a specific characteristic or function. Human chromosomes contain between 50 and 250 million base pairs of nucleotides. Genes contain the hereditary instructions that control the production of certain proteins. It is the proper

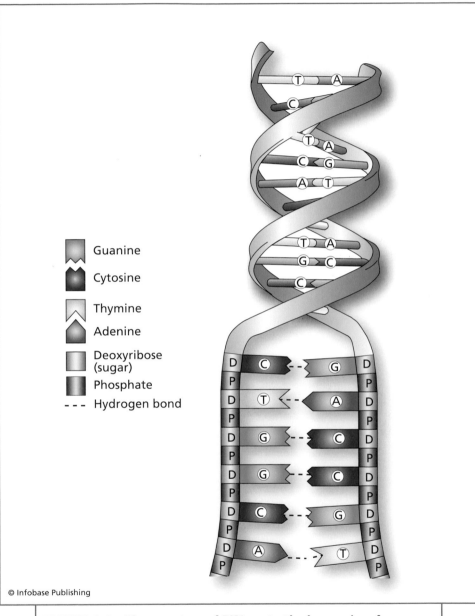

Guanine

Cytosine

Thymine

Adenine

Deoxyribose (sugar)

Phosphate

- - - Hydrogen bond

FIGURE 8.1   The structure of DNA; note the base pairs of nucleotides that make up the "rungs" of the ladder.

production of proteins that enables an organism to function correctly.

All the cells of an organism have the same number of chromosomes in the nucleus except for sperm and eggs, which are the sex cells. In humans, all body cells, or autosomes, contain 46 chromosomes. Human sex cells contain half that number (23 chromosomes), so that when the

CHROMOSOME NUMBERS IN DIFFERENT ORGANISMS

Biologists have found no apparent significance in the number of chromosomes an organism has and the type of organism. Note, for example, that humans have fewer chromosomes than single-celled amoebas or tobacco plants.

Organism	Number of Chromosomes
Onion	16
Redwood tree	22
Grasshopper	24
Bullfrog	26
Alligator	32
Holly	40
Sea urchin	42
Human	46
Tobacco plant	48
Amoeba	50
Cow	60
Guinea pig	64
Magnolia tree	76
Chicken	78
Whitefish	80

sperm nucleus and egg nucleus fuse at fertilization, the full chromosome number, 46, is restored. The cell produced by fertilization is the first cell of the new organism, and it has the full chromosome number.

In sexually reproducing organisms, including humans, the offspring receives half of its chromosomes from the father's sperm and half from the mother's egg. In this way, the offspring **inherits** from both parents the genes that ultimately give it its unique characteristics.

As the **embryo** grows inside the mother (in mammals), the cells divide and begin to differentiate to form different tissues and organs. When cells divide, the chromosomes must first be duplicated so that each new cell can receive the full number in the process called *mitosis*. For example, as human cells divide, the 46 chromosomes are duplicated (to make 96 chromosomes). The double set of chromosomes separates, and one full set of 46 chromosomes moves to one side of the cell and the other full set of 46 chromosomes moves to the other side of the cell. The cell then pinches in across its middle, producing two cells, each with the full number of 46 chromosomes.

Basic to the process of cell division described above is the duplication, or **replication**, of the DNA molecules in the chromosomes. For the organism to be normal and healthy, every pair of nucleotides in the new DNA molecules must be exactly the same as in the originals. The enzyme DNA polymerase functions in the accurate replication of DNA.

While DNA is located in the cell's nucleus, the actual proteins specified by genes are made by components called **ribosomes,** which are located in the **cytoplasm.** The transfer of the genetic information from the genes in the nucleus to the ribosomes involves another kind of nucleic acid, **ribonucleic acid,** or **RNA**. RNA, like DNA, is made up of nucleotides, but with a few differences. First, the sugar in

RNA is ribose instead of deoxyribose, and second, instead of thymine (T), RNA contains a base called uracil (U), which pairs with adenine (A). Also, RNA is a single-stranded molecule, while a DNA molecule consists of two strands bonded together. RNA functions in protein synthesis, using information from the DNA in the cell nucleus.

The hereditary information in the genes is present in the specific sequence of nucleotides in the DNA molecules. This information is copied into a molecule of a type of RNA called messenger RNA, or mRNA, in a process called **transcription**. In transcription, the nucleotide sequence of the gene is copied into the nucleotide sequence of the mRNA. The mRNA then crosses the nuclear membrane and enters the cytoplasm.

It sometimes happens that errors occur in the replication or transcription of DNA. Such errors are called **mutations**. Mutations occur when there is an error in the sequence of nucleotides. Mutations can also involve pieces of or whole chromosomes. The following are five types of mutations in genes and chromosomes:

1. Point mutations, in which a base pair in a DNA molecule is replaced by another base pair;
2. Deletions, in which one or more base pairs is missing from a nucleotide sequence of a DNA molecule;
3. Insertions, in which one or more base pairs is added to a nucleotide sequence of a DNA molecule;
4. Translocations, in which a piece of one chromosome moves to a new location on another chromosome;
5. Inversions, in which part of a chromosome breaks off and then reattaches, but turned upside down.

IDENTIFYING GENES

The Human Genome Project was charged with the enormous task of identifying all 3 billion nucleotide pairs found in the DNA of human chromosomes. Why did the scientists attempt to identify the nucleotide sequences of all the genes? Knowledge of the human genome will eventually allow scientists to learn where each gene is located on which chromosome and what each gene does (what protein it produces). Such knowledge will be of enormous importance in dealing with the genetic aspects of all sorts of diseases.

Knowledge of the normal nucleotide sequence also allows researchers to recognize abnormal, or mutant, genes. If scientists did not know that, for example, a correct gene sequence in one spot on a particular chromosome is A-T T-A C-G, they would never figure out that the gene sequence A-T A-T C-G in that location is a mutation. A mutant gene may result in the production of an abnormal, nonfunctional protein. For example, the gene sequence A-T T-A C-G may code for a protein that the cell needs to survive. If the mutant gene sequence—A-T A-T C-G—produces a nonfunctional protein, disease or death could result.

How do scientists identify and analyze the genes on tiny bits of DNA? In one method of gene identification, called gene sequencing, the DNA sample is divided into four parts. A nucleic acid strand called a primer, which serves as a starting point for DNA replication, is added to each part. Each part is then treated with a special nucleotide that stops DNA replication. That strand of DNA replicates itself until it reaches the special nucleotide, and then replication stops. If the termination nucleotide was a G nucleotide, which is always paired with a C nucleotide, scientists know that at the spot where the DNA stopped replicating there must be

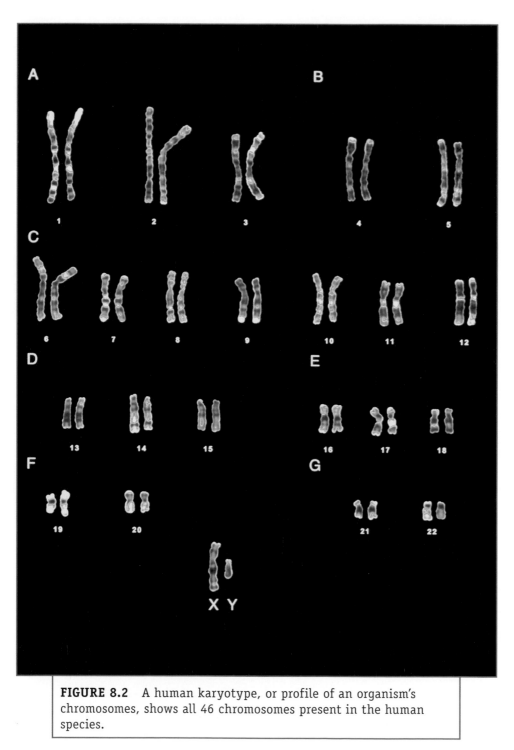

FIGURE 8.2 A human karyotype, or profile of an organism's chromosomes, shows all 46 chromosomes present in the human species.

a C nucleotide. The scientists record this spot on their DNA "map" with a C. This rather tedious process, which thankfully is done with the help of machines and computers, continues until every nucleotide on the DNA strand is noted, or sequenced.

Analytical processes like this allowed scientists to identify and sequence every nucleotide in the human genome. By 2003, scientists had a very good idea of the normal sequence of human genes. Once the normal sequence was known, medical researchers could turn their attention to finding gene mutations that cause disease or are implicated in disease.

Genes and Inheritance

Like all sexually reproducing organisms, humans get half of their genes from their father and half of their genes from their mother. Therefore, there are two genes for every trait, or characteristic—one from the father and one from the mother. Some traits are expressed (appear) in the offspring whenever the gene for that trait is passed on from one parent. For example, most people have dimples. A child will have dimples if he or she gets only one "dimples" gene from either his or her mother or his or her father. That is because the gene that causes the formation of dimples is a **dominant gene**. The gene for no dimples is a **recessive gene**. The recessive trait is hidden when the dominant gene is present.

The recessive trait appears only in individuals who have two copies of the recessive gene. The trait is hidden whenever the dominant gene is present. For example, cystic fibrosis afflicts only those children who inherit two cystic fibrosis genes, one from their mother and one from their father. If the child gets only one cystic fibrosis gene from one parent, then the child does not get the disease.

There is a simple diagram that shows the genetic makeup of possible offspring if the genetic makeup of the parents is known. This diagram is called a Punnett square. In a Punnett square, the genes for a particular trait from each parent are shown in boxes. When making a Punnett square, a capital letter is used for the dominant gene, and the lowercase form of the same letter is used for the recessive gene. In books, the names and abbreviations for genes are typically shown in italic type.

The Punnett square below shows one way that children could inherit dimples from their two parents. *D* stands for the dominant dimples gene; *d* stands for the recessive "no dimples" gene.

In this case, the mother has two recessive genes for dimples (*dd*), and she herself has no dimples. Since the mother has only the recessive gene, her children will inherit one copy of the recessive gene. The father, on the other hand, has two dominant genes for dimples (*DD*), and he does have dimples. Since the father has only the dominant gene, all of his children will inherit one copy of the dominant gene.

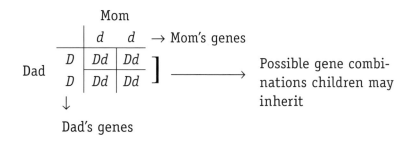

In this case, any child that this couple has will inherit dimples from the father.

The next Punnett squares show the likelihood of a child getting cystic fibrosis when only one parent carries the recessive gene (left) or when both parents carry the recessive gene (right). *H* stands for no cystic fibrosis gene; *h* stands for the recessive cystic fibrosis gene.

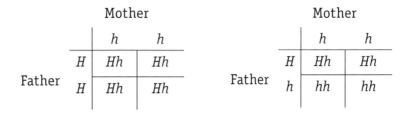

In the case where only one parent has the recessive gene, none of the children inherits two recessive genes (*hh*). Instead, they all inherit only one recessive gene (*Hh*), so they do not get the disease. In the case where both parents have a recessive gene (even if only one), there is a 50% chance that a child may inherit two recessive genes (*hh*) and be born with cystic fibrosis.

Understanding how genes are inherited is important for understanding how genes may cause diseases such as Parkinson's.

THE GENETIC BASIS OF PARKINSON'S

One of the earliest and largest studies ever conducted to see if there was a genetic cause for Parkinson's disease followed all the male identical and fraternal twin brothers who had served in the U.S. armed forces during World War II. (Identical twins arise from the division of a single fertilized egg cell; they therefore have the same genetic material. Fraternal twins arise from the simultaneous fertilization of two egg cells by two different sperm; they therefore share about 50% of their genes, just like other siblings.) Among the large group of identical twins, the researchers identified about 70 men who had developed Parkinson's disease. The researchers figured that because identical twins have identical genes, if one brother had Parkinson's, his genetically identical twin would also have it. However,

Parkinson's was found to occur in pairs of identical twins in only 16% of the cases studied. This was not significantly different from the 11% of nonidentical twins in the study who both had Parkinson's, even though they did not share the same genes.[16] This study led many medical researchers to conclude that there was no genetic basis for Parkinson's disease.

Some researchers questioned this conclusion. They pointed out several situations in which genes might still be implicated in Parkinson's disease. For example, critics claimed that some genes do not cause a disease by themselves, but require an environmental "jump start" before the disease develops. Perhaps, in the above study, one identical twin worked on a farm and was exposed to pesticides, while the other identical twin lived and worked in a city. Both may have had the same gene that predisposed them to Parkinson's, but only the twin exposed to pesticides, a known risk factor for Parkinson's, developed the disease.

Another argument points out that Parkinson's disease usually starts fairly late in life. It is possible that some of the identical twins died before they developed full-blown Parkinson's. In the era before sophisticated brain scans, it was not possible for researchers to determine if one or both identical twin brothers had observable changes to the substantia nigra. Remember that Parkinson's symptoms do not usually appear until about 80% of the substantia nigra neurons have died. It is possible that some of the identical twin pairs did have Parkinson's, but it was undiagnosed in one or both of them.

All in all, twin studies left too many questions unanswered and variables unaddressed. They did not make clear whether or not there was a genetic factor in Parkinson's disease, whether environmental factors affected expression of a Parkinson's gene (if there was one), or if Parkinson's was inherited.

Family Matters

Several centuries ago, a Greek family moved from their native Greece to the beautiful town of Contursi in southern Italy. For many years, the family prospered and grew to include several hundred members. In about 1700, two related individuals in this family got married. Soon, they started a family. Over the generations, it became clear that the descendants of this one couple showed a distinct susceptibility to what is now known to be Parkinson's disease.

Between 1900 and 1920, several members of this Italian family left Italy and moved to the United States. Doctors found that an unusually large number of individuals in this family—both in the United States and in Italy—developed what by then could definitely be diagnosed as Parkinson's disease. Researchers in the two countries worked together to find out why so many members of this family developed this disease. The Italian researchers traced the family's history back 12 generations and identified nearly 600 members. Of course, it was impossible to get health histories for individuals who lived hundreds of years ago, but the Italian doctors did get histories for the last four generations of family members. The researchers found that in only the last 4 generations, 61 members of this family had Parkinson's disease. Doctors in the United States and in Italy determined that these family members had true Parkinson's disease and not a form of parkinsonism. They also found that fully 40% of the family members over 50 years old developed Parkinson's.[17]

Researchers on both sides of the Atlantic began to make detailed genetic studies of every living member of this family. The genetic studies revealed a clear pattern of inheritance of Parkinson's. The results of the study showed that, in this family at least, Parkinson's disease was caused by a mutation in a non-sex cell dominant gene. In genetics, this is called an **autosomal dominant disease**.

Several years after this study was completed, other familial patterns of Parkinson's disease were found and studied. Researchers at the Mayo Clinic in Minnesota followed all the members of one family in Iowa for several generations. They found that 22 members of the family developed Parkinson's disease. Other families with seemingly inherited Parkinson's were found and studied in the United States, Germany, and Denmark. The unmistakable family pattern of the disease led to renewed interest in finding the gene or genes that caused the disease. Gene sequencing made the search for Parkinson's genes possible.

Identifying Genes

Genetic sequencing enabled researchers to narrow their search for the genes that cause Parkinson's. By 1996, it became clear that the genes associated with Parkinson's code for specific proteins that control vital brain chemicals. Genetic mutations result in the production of abnormal proteins that do not work correctly. In particular, the mutant genes cause the creation of abnormal forms of the proteins alpha synuclein, parkin, and ubiquitin carboxy-terminal hydrolase. All three of these proteins are vital for ridding brain cells of accumulated substances that would otherwise harm them. When these "garbage disposal" proteins are abnormal (because the genes that code for them are mutant), harmful material builds up in brain cells, and the brain cells may be unable to function or may die.

Using genetic material from the Italian-American family described above, geneticists (scientists who study genes) were able to identify a dominant autosomal gene that codes for the production of the protein alpha synuclein. In this family, the gene had a mutation that disabled the protein and caused a buildup of harmful material in brain cells, particularly the cells of the substantia nigra. Researchers have since located this mutated gene, called the alpha synuclein gene, on chromosome 4.

Identifying this gene was a major breakthrough, though at that time scientists had very little idea what alpha synuclein actually did and how its malfunction led to Parkinson's. Today, researchers know that alpha synuclein is a protein that is normally present in all brain cells, especially in the axon terminals of neurons. After developing a stain that enables scientists to see this protein in cells, researchers began looking for it during autopsies of patients who had had noninherited Parkinson's. They were astounded by what they found—alpha synuclein was the major component of Lewy bodies. Thus, Parkinson's sufferers who did *not* have a mutant gene still had alpha synuclein in their brain cells and Lewy bodies. So there were two avenues—one hereditary and one not—that led to the same result.

Further investigations of U.S. families with inherited Parkinson's revealed new insights. One family had been identified as having a dominant gene inheritance pattern for the disease. Genetic analysis showed that the mutation arose from a gene duplication error. Members of this family had two genes for alpha synuclein production. It seems that overproduction of this protein caused it to accumulate in brain cells and Lewy bodies.

The role of alpha synuclein in Parkinson's is a subject of intense research. Most Parkinson's patients do not have a mutated gene, yet they have excessive alpha synuclein in their brain cells and Lewy bodies. Scientists have made some interesting discoveries regarding this protein. For instance, alpha synuclein usually dissolves easily in cell fluids. However, under certain circumstances, it becomes insoluble and actually forms clumps, which often stick together and form larger clumps. Neurons have a particularly hard time getting rid of clumpy alpha synuclein, so it tends to accumulate in the cells. If enough clumpy alpha synuclein accumulates, brain cells may be unable to function or may die. Exactly what causes alpha synuclein to act this way is not fully understood.

Other protein-coding genes have been implicated in Parkinson's disease. Japanese researchers have been following families in which early onset Parkinson's is common. In these families, members were diagnosed with parkinsonism by age 20. The inheritance pattern in these families showed that the disease did not continue from one generation to the next (as in the Italian-American family), but was restricted to a single generation at a time, often skipping several generations. This indicated that the cause was likely a recessive gene. When the Japanese researchers identified this recessive gene, they named it *parkin*.[18]

Parkin is a protein that is present in all brain cells. Its job is to dispose of other accumulated proteins that brain cells need to get rid of. Parkin is just one part of a complex metabolic system in brain cells called the ubiquitin-protease system. This system removes from brain cells the used-up or abnormal proteins that the neuron needs to have hauled away. This system breaks down these useless or damaged proteins into tiny bits that the cell can then easily expel. Thus, Parkinson's disease is associated with genetic mutations that cause the brain to have either too much protein (alpha synuclein) or an abnormal protein (parkin) that cannot dispose of other used-up proteins.

However, things are not as simple as that. Additional research has turned up yet another mutant gene that is likely associated with Parkinson's. The *UCHL1* gene controls the system in the brain that recycles ubiquitin. The normal gene "unglues" ubiquitin from the chemical complex it is a part of (ubiquitin carboxy-terminal hydrolase) so it can be used again. If this gene is mutated, the ubiquitin is not freed up and recycled. Eventually, there is not enough ubiquitin available for "trash removal" from brain cells, and neurons begin accumulating dangerous levels of "trash."

Another interesting bit of the puzzle reveals that one of the key proteins removed by a normal ubiquitin complex is alpha synuclein. Thus, when the ubiquitin-recycling gene is mutant, not only does ubiquitin become scarce, but alpha synuclein accumulates in brain cells. Today, many Parkinson's researchers are concentrating their efforts on the ubiquitin-protease system and on the proteins— particularly alpha synuclein—that the system breaks down and discards.

Causes or Conditions?

Geneticists have learned that there are several different normal forms of the *UCHL1* gene. Different normal forms of the same gene are referred to as **polymorphisms**. Polymorphism is more the rule than the exception when it comes to human genes. The fascinating fact found by Parkinson's researchers, however, was that people who had a specific polymorphic form of the *UCHL1* gene (a form called *S18Y*) had a much lower risk (50% lower) of developing Parkinson's disease than individuals with other normal forms of the gene. Polymorphisms in the alpha synuclein gene have revealed similar results. One form of the alpha synuclein gene, called *Rep1*, is found in both normal people and people with Parkinson's.[19] Yet people with Parkinson's are far more likely to be carrying the *Rep1* form of the gene than people who do not have the disease. In other words, it seems that having certain polymorphic forms of certain genes predisposes a person to getting Parkinson's disease.

This genetic predisposition to getting Parkinson's was also borne out in the Japanese studies of young adults with *parkin* gene mutations. The researchers knew that young adults who had two mutated recessive *parkin* genes developed Parkinson's disease. What, they wondered, happened to family members who inherited only one mutant recessive gene? These family members did not automatically get early onset Parkinson's, but did having one recessive gene predispose them to Parkinson's later in life? Though studies are ongoing, initial results indicate that the presence of one recessive defective gene makes these individuals more susceptible to developing Parkinson's disease in later life. The presence of one mutant *parkin* gene appears to be a risk factor for developing Parkinson's disease, especially if the individual is exposed to causative environmental conditions.

To sum up, in some relatively rare family cases, the inheritance of mutant genes does lead to Parkinson's. A large body of evidence shows that more often, genetic factors predispose a person to developing Parkinson's disease. How closely related this predisposition is to environmental factors is unclear. Yet there are still numerous questions and mysteries surrounding the genes that have already been implicated in Parkinson's, as well as newly discovered genetic mutations that are believed to be associated with the disease. What role do these genes play in Parkinson's disease? Are there still more genes implicated as well? Researchers are pursuing answers to these questions.

New evidence of genetic connections in Parkinson's disease was reported in 2006. European researchers discovered that certain ethnic groups had unusually high incidences of a single mutation in a protein-coding gene, called leucine-rich repeat kinase gene, or *LRRK2*. This gene was first identified in 2004 in families that had a history of inherited autosomal dominant Parkinson's disease. The scientists reportedly found strong evidence that the newly discovered mutation, called *G2019S*, in the *LRRK2* gene is closely associated with Parkinson's disease. The researchers also found that people who have the *G2019S* mutation also often have a mutated *parkin* gene.[20] Researchers from the Mayo Clinic announced that they had identified one type of mutation in the alpha synuclein gene that increases people's risk of developing Parkinson's disease. The investigators determined that the DNA segment that contains

SOME GENES IMPLICATED IN PARKINSON'S DISEASE

GENE	LOCATION ON CHROMOSOME	LOCUS	MODE OF INHERITANCE	NUMBER OF KNOWN MUTATIONS
alpha synuclein	4q21.3	PARK1	autosomal dominant	5
parkin	6q25.2-27	PARK2	autosomal recessive	108
UCHL1 (ubiquitin carboxy-terminal hydrolase)	4p14	PARK5	autosomal dominant	3
LRRK2	12p11.2-q13.1	PARK8	autosomal dominant	20

Note: *Locus* refers to the place on the chromosome where the specific gene is located; *p* and *q* refer to the length of the chromosome "arm"; *p* indicates a gene on the short arm of the chromosome; *q* indicates a gene of the long arm of a chromosome.

the alpha synuclein gene is noticeably longer in people who get the disease than in normal people. This finding may lead to the development of treatments focused on reducing the length of this gene segment by using drugs that inhibit overexpression of the alpha synuclein gene.[21] Table 1 summarizes information about the genes that have been implicated in Parkinson's disease.

A Future for Gene Therapy?

Gene therapy utilizes techniques that can alter or replace defective or mutant genes. For example, as described previously, an enzyme might be developed that is able to "snip" off the extra length in a mutant alpha synuclein gene to allow that gene to function properly.

All forms of gene therapy for Parkinson's disease are still in the experimental stage. Many approaches are being tested. For example, genes that code for the production of dopamine have been inserted into the brain cells of test animals to induce greater dopamine production. A great deal of research currently under way is testing viruses for delivery of healthy genes. In this procedure, a healthy gene is inserted into to the harmless virus's DNA, and the genetically altered virus is introduced into the body. Viruses work by invading the body's cells, such as neurons, and forcing them to reproduce the virus's DNA. If the virus's DNA contains healthy human genes, these healthy genes are incorporated into the DNA of the neuron. Thus, the neuron's mutated DNA is

(opposite) **FIGURE 8.3**   One form of gene therapy involves the insertion of normal genes into the DNA of a patient's cells. Viruses carry the healthy gene to the cells of the body.

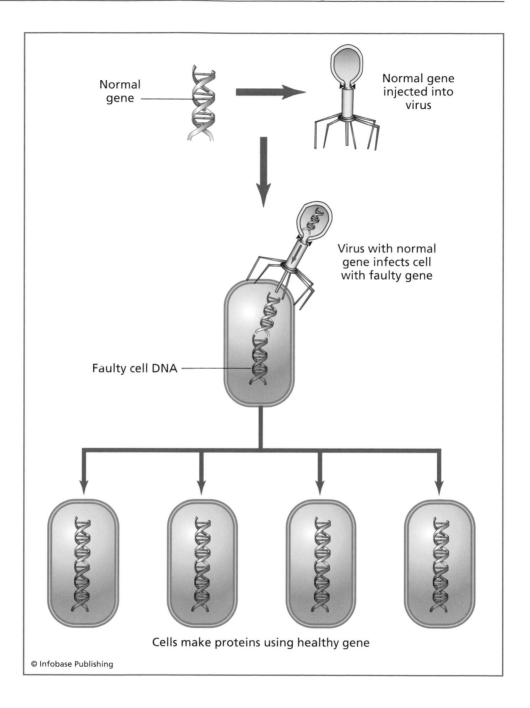

Normal
gene

Normal gene
injected into
virus

Virus with normal
gene infects cell
with faulty gene

Faulty cell DNA

Cells make proteins using healthy gene

reprogrammed with healthy genes that properly produce or control brain proteins.

In another type of genetic research, scientists are removing living cells from the body of Parkinson's patients and altering their genes. For example, researchers harvest bone marrow cells and alter them by inserting the normal, non-mutated form of the damaged neurological gene into the DNA. Then the living cells, carrying the normal form of the gene, are injected into the brain of the Parkinson's patient. Because the cells come from the patient's own body, they are not rejected by the immune system (see Chapter 9). The healthy genes can begin to code for the normal production of the proteins implicated in Parkinson's disease.

Gene therapy is still highly experimental, and no tried-and-true therapy has yet been devised. Still, it is one promising approach to correcting the genetic mutations associated with Parkinson's disease.

9

FUTURE TREATMENTS—OR CURES

Researchers are learning more about Parkinson's disease every year, and the fight against Parkinson's is being fought on many fronts. For example, the science of protein chemistry is one of the most exciting fields of research today. Scientists know that genes code for protein production and that proteins enable organisms to function. Therefore, researchers are looking for ways to alter defective proteins to treat diseases caused by genetic abnormalities. One day, they may find a way to treat Parkinson's sufferers with the normal protein that controls metabolism of alpha synuclein or one of the other proteins or enzymes implicated in the disease.

Other avenues of research show great promise for treating or curing Parkinson's disease. One of the most promising methods is also one of the most controversial. Some of the most recent fields of Parkinson's research are reviewed in this chapter.

CELL IMPLANTATION

One experimental technique for treating Parkinson's involves the implantation of neurons that produce dopamine.

In one approach, cells that release a specific neurotransmitter that activates dopamine-secreting neurons are implanted in the brain, in or near the corpus striatum. One drawback to this treatment thus far is that it generally does not generate the creation of synaptic connections among neurons. In some experimental techniques, the neurotransmitter-releasing cells have been able to create only a limited number of synaptic connections in the immediate vicinity of the implantation, and few or none beyond it.

The first surgeries done to implant cells in the brain took place in the mid-1980s. Cells were removed from one of the patient's adrenal glands, some of whose tissues produce dopamine and similar substances. The adrenal cells were implanted in the patient's striatum. These initial attempts at cell implantation had a very poor success rate. Most Parkinson's patients showed little or no improvement. When the patients in these trials died, their brains were studied at autopsy. Autopsies revealed that none of the patients had any surviving adrenal cells in their brain. It seems that the treatment did not work, because the implanted adrenal cells could not survive and function in the brain.

Doctors wondered if perhaps the problem was that the adrenal cells were too old to learn to survive in a new environment. Or perhaps the adrenal cells were nearing the end of their normal lifespan and simply died in the brain. After all, most Parkinson's patients are relatively elderly—and so are their body cells. Physicians concluded that using very young and healthy cells might do the trick. Where would such cells come from? Beginning in the 1990s, doctors tried harvesting fetal brain cells from naturally miscarried fetuses. Again, though, implants of these fetal brain cells yielded disappointing results. In one study, slight improvement in symptoms occurred only in patients over 60 years old. Another study showed that only patients with very mild symptoms were slightly improved. Both studies revealed a disturbing increase in dyskinesia in all implanted patients.[22] Given the difficulty obtaining fetal brain cells, this approach was abandoned.

One major problem with implantation is immune system rejection of foreign cells. Rejection occurs for all implants or transplants of cells, tissues, or organs that come from another person (other than an identical twin). The job of the immune system is to identify, attack, and destroy foreign cells and materials in the body. Decades of research and experience with transplantation of organs, such as kidneys and hearts, have led to the development of drugs that effectively suppress the immune response. Unfortunately, these drugs leave the entire immune system suppressed, so that the patient becomes more vulnerable to disease. Immunosuppressant drugs might also be used in Parkinson's patients who get cell implantation. One positive aspect of brain-cell implantation, however, is that the immune system is not as active in the brain as it is in other parts of the body. It is possible that a person who gets brain-cell implants might not need any immunosuppressant drugs or might be able to make do with a low dose.

HORMONES AND GENES

Neurotrophic hormones, hormones that stimulate nerve growth, nourish brain cells and make them healthier. In some cases, it has been found that neurotrophic hormones can coax existing brain cells into creating new synaptic connections. One neurotrophic hormone that is the focus of intense research is called glial cell line–derived neurotrophic factor (GDNF). GDNF is a powerful growth factor for dopamine-producing cells in the brain.

The first clinical trials using GDNF introduced the hormone directly into the brain through a permanently inserted tube. This technique did not work well. It was the delivery method of choice because GDNF cannot cross the blood-brain barrier. Furthermore, GDNF and other neurotrophic hormones are quickly broken down and disposed of in the brain. Even worse, these chemicals do not travel through the brain to the desired site, so they must be inserted directly into or near the target cells. Some researchers have been experimenting with inserting genes that code for production of these hormones into the DNA of harmless viruses. They hope that one day these viruses can be introduced into the brain, take up residence in brain cells, and get the

GENETIC SCREENING

Genetic screening—the testing of an individual or group of people to see if they carry a particular gene or genes—enables scientists to tell people if they have disease-causing genes that their children might inherit. Such analysis exists for diseases caused by recessive genes, such as cystic fibrosis or Tay-Sachs disease. As scientists continue to find genes that are implicated in Parkinson's disease, genetic analysis may enable them to predict which individuals have a genetic predisposition for Parkinson's. Genetic analysis would also allow doctors to determine which members in those rare families carry a dominant gene that causes Parkinson's in offspring. Once the genes that make a person susceptible to Parkinson's are identified, medications could possibly prevent the disease from developing (for instance, by degrading accumulating proteins in the brain) or relieve its symptoms and keep it in check (for example, using medications that induce dopamine production).

substantia nigra or striatum cells of Parkinson's patients to make GDNF and similar hormones.

Another complicating factor is that there are a huge number of neurotrophic hormones, each responsible for one tiny part of one small mechanism within a normally functioning brain. In fact, scientists are learning that each type of neuron has its own entire family or subfamily of neurotrophic hormones. The exceeding complexity of isolating, or correctly combining, just the right hormone or hormones to treat Parkinson's disease is keeping many medical researchers very busy indeed. To date, no GDNF therapy has been developed for Parkinson's, but the prospects may improve as scientists untangle this knotty problem.

Genetic Programming and Cloning

Geneticists have identified a gene on human chromosome 11 that codes for the dopamine receptor on brain neurons. This gene can now be **cloned**, or copied exactly, in the laboratory. Researchers have also been able to analyze dopamine receptor proteins in amazing detail. One day soon, a drug may be developed that utilizes these proteins to activate and reinvigorate dopamine receptors on brain cells, or a healthy cloned gene might be introduced into damaged neurons to get them to replicate healthy genes that code for dopamine production.

In another approach, diseased brain cells could be surgically removed from the patient. The neurons' DNA could be genetically reprogrammed with a healthy gene and then reinserted into the brain. These genetically transformed cells would then begin to function properly because they would have healthy genes for the production or reception of dopamine, for production and disposal of alpha synuclein, or for correction of any other error that leads to Parkinson's or its symptoms. Using a virus to transport the healthy genes might be an alternative method that makes surgery unnecessary.

Researchers are also experimenting with removing a patient's own bone marrow cells and inserting healthy genes into them. Bone marrow cells reproduce more frequently than most body cells, so they would make many cells that contain the healthy gene. These bone marrow cells could then be injected into the brain of the person with Parkinson's. The beauty of this method is that there would be no rejection problem, because the bone marrow cells would come from the patient being treated.

Stem Cells

When a sperm fertilizes an egg, the single cell begins to divide and forms an embryo, an organism in its early stages of development prior to birth. By the time the embryo contains about 150 cells, the group of cells is a ball called a **blastocyst**. Some cells that make up a blastocyst—called **embryonic stem cells**—are very special. They are undifferentiated and have the potential to turn into any type of body cell. As the embryo develops, different blastocyst cells begin to differentiate. Some begin to form bones, others to form the heart and circulatory system, others to form muscles, others to form the cells of the central nervous system (including the brain), and so on.

A blastocyst is extremely tiny—smaller than the period at the end of this sentence. As the **stem cells** in the blastocyst start to specialize to become particular cell types, they divide many, many times to create the billions of cells that make up the tissues and organs of the organism. Special regions on DNA act as triggers that instruct undifferentiated blastocyst cells to develop into particular kinds of cells. After a long series of cell divisions, the blastocyst cells are said to be "terminally differentiated." At this point, they have become the type of cell they will always be, and they can never become a different type of cell. For example, at this stage, a blastocyst cell that has differentiated to become a bone cell will forevermore be a bone cell.

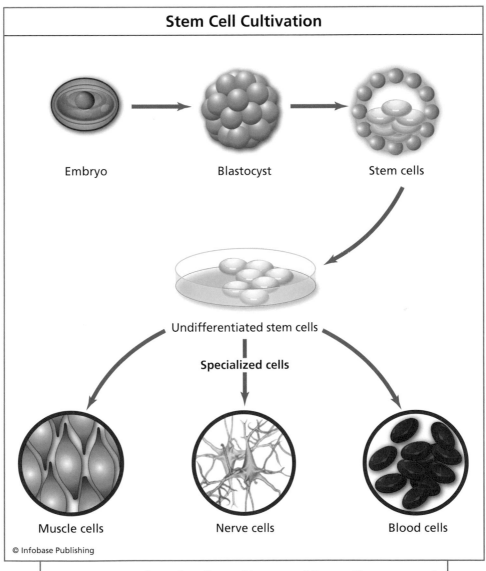

Stem Cell Cultivation

Embryo   Blastocyst   Stem cells

Undifferentiated stem cells

Specialized cells

Muscle cells   Nerve cells   Blood cells

© Infobase Publishing

FIGURE 9.1 Embryonic cells can be removed from a blastocyst and grown in a Petri dish in a lab. These undifferentiated stem cells can then be grown to form any type of body cell, including neurons.

Embryonic stem cells have enormous potential for treating diseases such as Parkinson's. Scientists hope that undifferentiated stem cells can be coaxed into becoming any type of healthy cell needed to treat a particular disease. For example, scientists are finding ways to get undifferentiated embryonic stem cells to become brain cells. Parkinson's researchers may soon be able to induce undifferentiated embryonic stem cells to become healthy substantia nigra or striatum neurons. These healthy neurons could then be inserted into the brains of people with Parkinson's disease, where they would begin to multiply and take over the normal production of dopamine. Healthy neurons that properly control the production of brain enzymes and the elimination of proteins could also be inserted into the brains of Parkinson's patients.

Another positive aspect of embryonic stem cell treatment is that the body being treated does not seem to reject these transformed stem cells. Experiments in animals have shown that the immune system is not activated to fight introduced embryonic stem cells.

Controversy

There is a huge debate swirling around the use of embryonic stem cells to treat disease. The debate arises from the source of these cells. Embryonic stem cells come from human embryos created at fertility clinics.

Couples who have difficulty conceiving a child may go to a fertility clinic for treatment. At the clinic, some of the woman's eggs are surgically removed from her ovaries and placed in a test tube. The man's sperm is added, and many of the eggs are fertilized and form embryos. This artificial process is called **in vitro fertilization** because it takes place outside the body (as opposed to in vivo, which means "inside the body"). Because this type of fertilization is often difficult to achieve, many eggs and sperm are united to form many embryos. This assures that there are at least as many embryos as the couple seeking treatment can use. The doctors monitor the fertilized eggs and then implant one or more embryos into the woman's uterus, where, hopefully, it will develop into a baby.

Many extra embryos remain at the clinic. These embryos are made up of blastocysts with undifferentiated stem cells. These undifferentiated stem cells are the main source of embryonic stem cells used in medical research. Medical researchers are able to use certain techniques to induce some of these undifferentiated embryonic stem cells into becoming different kinds of healthy body cells. Embryonic stem cells are especially useful for finding treatments for neurological diseases such as Parkinson's because neurons do not (or very rarely) reproduce. Unlike other types of body cells that reproduce and replace themselves all the time—skin cells, for example—neurons generally do not regenerate.

The ethical dilemma surrounding embryonic stem cells arises from people's different definitions of what a human person is. People who oppose embryonic stem cell research claim that a fertilized human egg and a blastocyst are human—as human as a living child or adult. Thus, they oppose using this human being (the blastocyst) for research or for healing another person, because the blastocyst is destroyed in the process. Opponents of embryonic stem cell research firmly believe that this is not moral and should not be done.

People who support embryonic stem cell research claim that an embryo or a blastocyst is not a human being, but only a cluster of cells. To be a true human person, they say, the embryo's cells must at least have already differentiated. Embryonic stem cell research supporters certainly acknowledge that these stem cells have the potential to become a human person, but only if they are implanted in a woman's uterus and develop into a baby. As it is, because so many extra embryos are created at fertility clinics, to make sure that at least one will "take," most of them will eventually be destroyed. (It is very expensive to keep these embryos alive, so after a while—usually after the birth of the baby—they are discarded.) Supporters of this research feel strongly that it is far more important to use embryonic stem cells to alleviate the suffering of living people than to deny them the chance to have their disease successfully treated or cured in order to save a blastocyst.

Embryonic stem cell research is a thorny problem with no clear or absolute solution. People on both sides believe strongly in their point of view. In most Western nations, except for the United States, the ethical dilemma has been resolved in favor of embryonic stem cell research. In Europe, embryonic stem cell research is yielding valuable insights into and possible treatments or cures for a number of neurological diseases, including Parkinson's, and for brain and spinal cord injury, as well as for diseases such as diabetes. Only in the United States has embryonic stem cell research been severely limited, and this limitation has hobbled medical research.

On September 28, 1999, and again on September 14, 2000, Michael J. Fox appeared before a U.S. Senate subcommittee to call for federal funds for embryonic stem cell research. The following is a brief excerpt of Fox's 2000 testimony.

> For two years, you've had a parade of witnesses, scientists, ethicists, theologians of every school, and some celebrities, discussing every nuance of stem cell research. You've given time to all sides of the issue. . . . But the inescapable conclusion is that this research offers a potential to

eliminate diseases, [to] literally save millions of lives. . . . [Experts show that] Parkinson's would be one of the first diseases to benefit from the use of stem cells. . . . Now a major scientific breakthrough has given us the opportunity to uphold [a] principle of our government to do the greatest good for the greatest number of people. I'm referring, of course, to the recent discovery of the miraculous potential of stem cells. . . . I see in these cells a chance for a medical miracle. The government has done its work. We ask you now to release our tax dollars so the scientists can do theirs.[23]

Because of resistance to embryonic stem cell research in the United States, American scientists are trying to determine whether adult cells can be used instead. Adults have a type of stem cell in their bone marrow. These bone marrow stem cells can be reprogrammed to make other body cells. There are, however, two drawbacks in terms of Parkinson's research. One disadvantage of bone marrow stem cells is that so far it seems that they are very difficult, perhaps impossible, to turn into healthy, functioning neurons. Another negative is that bone marrow cells do not multiply as quickly as embryonic stem cells. Embryonic stem cells multiply very rapidly, which makes them very useful in producing lots of needed neurons. Mature bone marrow stem cells may not multiply fast enough to produce the number of neurons needed to compensate for the loss of substantia nigra cells in Parkinson's patients (or for regrowing nerve cells for people paralyzed by spinal cord injuries). Still, U.S. researchers are working with whatever they can get, or using private funding for embryonic stem cell research—though it is likely that it will be government-funded European scientists who will create and market exciting, new stem cell therapies.

In 2006, academic researchers announced that they had found and isolated an adult stem cell from blood that can be induced to turn into five types of body cells, including neurons. Though the adult stem cell is more limited in the number of body cells it can become (embryonic stem cells can become any type of cell), it is still an exciting development, because the blood stem cell can become a neuron. The scientists kept the adult blood stem cells alive and then used chemical triggers to induce them to become one of the five body cells, including neurons. None of the neurons created was found to contain abnormalities. This research was conducted using pig blood, so the investigators will next attempt to reproduce these results using human blood stem cells. This is an exciting advance in stem cell research that has the potential to help Parkinson's patients. It remains to be seen how it translates to adult human stem cells, but so far the results are promising.[24]

Cause and Cure?

The more researchers learn about Parkinson's disease, the more they are zeroing in on alpha synuclein as the primary suspect in causing it. Current Parkinson's research is following the path taken by Alzheimer's researchers. Alzheimer's disease afflicts older people who steadily lose their memory and other brain functions. Scientists found that Alzheimer's is most likely caused by the accumulation of a protein in the brain. Since identifying that protein (beta-amyloid), they have been developing a vaccine that would prevent the accumulation of the protein in the brain of Alzheimer's patients.

Parkinson's researchers are pursuing a similar vaccine for alpha synuclein. The Parkinson's vaccine would introduce a chemical into the brain that would break up clumps of alpha synuclein (or prevent its accumulation in the first place) so that neurons could easily get rid of it. If, in fact, it turns out that alpha synuclein is the primary cause of Parkinson's, a vaccine could be given to people who have had their DNA analyzed and show a propensity for developing the disease. The vaccine would prevent buildup of alpha synuclein in the brain. This would prevent Parkinson's from developing in people who are susceptible to it.

Recent research has revealed that exposure to the pesticide paraquat causes alpha synuclein to accumulate in the brain and leads to the onset of Parkinson's disease. Perhaps the pesticide triggers a defective gene that causes Parkinson's. In any case, scientists agree that a definite step forward in the fight against Parkinson's would be to reduce pesticide use and ban those pesticides that are directly linked with Parkinson's (or other neurological diseases).[25]

Researchers working on Parkinson's disease are also busy developing drugs for treating people who already have the disease. The medications they hope to develop would induce the brain to create chemicals that break down the protein "culprits" so they can be disposed of. Perhaps one day, Parkinson's disease will be conquered.

NOTES

Chapter 1: The Trembling Was the Message

1. Michael J. Fox, *Lucky Man*. New York: Hyperion, 2002, p. 1.

2. Fox, *Lucky Man*, p. 2.

3. Fox, *Lucky Man*, p. 4.

4. Fox, *Lucky Man*, p. 7.

5. Alvin Silverstein, et al., *Parkinson's Disease*. Berkeley Heights, N.J.: Enslow, 2002, p. 30.

6. William J. Weiner, et al., *Parkinson's Disease: A Complete Guide for Patients and Families*. Baltimore: Johns Hopkins University Press, 2001, p. 21.

7. Silverstein, *Parkinson's Disease*, p. 62.

Chapter 2: A Short History of Parkinson's Disease

8. James Parkinson. "An Essay on the Shaking Palsy." Journal of Neuropsychiatry & Clinical Neurosciences Web site. Available online. URL: http://neuro. psychiatryonline.org/cgi/ content/full/14/2/223.

9. Parkinson, "An Essay on the Shaking Palsy."

10. Silverstein, *Parkinson's Disease*, p. 16.

Chapter 5: Symptoms and the Disease Process

11. Silverstein, *Parkinson's Disease*, p. 39.

12. Silverstein, *Parkinson's Disease*, p. 43.

Chapter 7: Treatment of Parkinson's Disease

13. J. Eric Ahlskog, *The Parkinson's Disease Treatment Book*. New York: Oxford University Press, 2005, pp. 99–100.

14. Ahlskog, *The Parkinson's Disease Treatment Book*, p. 103.

15. Ahlskog, *The Parkinson's Disease Treatment Book*, p. 484.

Chapter 8: Looking for a Genetic Cause

16. Ahlskog, *The Parkinson's Disease Treatment Book*, p. 88.

17. Roger C. Duvoisin and Jacob Sage, *Parkinson's Disease: A Guide for Patient and Family*. Philadelphia: Lippincott Williams & Wilkins, 2001, pp. 157–158.

18. Ahlskog, *The Parkinson's Disease Treatment Book*, p. 92.

19. Ahlskog, *The Parkinson's Disease Treatment Book*, pp. 93–94.

20. Vincenzo Bonifati. "The LRRK2-G2019S Mutation: Opening a Novel Era in Parkinson's Disease Genetics." The Michael J. Fox Foundation for Parkinson's Research Web site. Available online. URL: http://www.michaeljfox.org/news/article.php?id=234.

21. Mayo Clinic Press Release. "Strong Evidence of a Genetic Risk Factor for Parkinson's Disease." The Michael J. Fox Foundation for Parkinson's Research Web site. Available online. URL: http://www.michaeljfox.org/news/article.php?id=239.

Chapter 9: Future Treatments—or Cures

22. Ahlskog, *The Parkinson's Disease Treatment Book*, pp. 492–493.

23. Transcript of Testimony by Michael J. Fox before the Senate Appropriations Committee, September 14, 2000. CNN.com Transcripts Web site. Available online. URL: http://transcripts.cnn.com/TRANSCRIPTS/0009/14/se.03.html.

24. "Researchers Grow Neural, Blood Vessel Cells from Adult Stem Cells." The Michael J. Fox Foundation for Parkinson's Research Web site. Available online. URL: http://www.michaeljfox.org/news/article.php?id=260.

25. Reuters, "Studies Line Up on Parkinson's-Pesticides Link." Press release available online at Scientific American Web site. URL: www.sciam.com/article.cfm?alias=studies-line-up-on-parkin&chanID=sa003.

GLOSSARY

Acetylcholine A chemical neurotransmitter released by neurons in the striatum and involved in many brain functions, including control of motor activity and memory; also plays a major role in muscle contraction in the body.

Amino acids The chemicals that are the basic building blocks of proteins.

Anatomist A scientist who studies the structure of organisms.

Anatomy The structure of organisms.

Anticholinergic Referring to drugs that block acetylcholine cell receptors.

Autonomic nervous system The part of the nervous system that works automatically, or independently of thought or will.

Autopsy Medical examination and analysis of a corpse.

Autosomal dominant disease A disease caused by a mutation in a dominant gene found in a body cell (a non-sex cell).

Axon The single long, threadlike extension from the cell body of a neuron; carries impulses away from the cell body to the axon terminals.

Axon terminal Structure at the end of the axon that releases neurotransmitters.

Blastocyst A group of about 150 cells that forms from a fertilized egg by cell division; some blastocyst cells are embryonic stem cells that can differentiate into any type of body cell.

Blood-brain barrier A lining around the blood vessels of the brain that prevents unwanted or potentially harmful substances from entering the brain via the bloodstream.

Brain stem The lowest part of the brain that is continuous with the spinal cord; part of the autonomic nervous system that controls breathing and other basic life processes.

Central nervous system The brain and spinal cord.

Cerebellum Part of the brain structure located above the brain stem that coordinates body movements.

Cerebral cortex The convoluted surface layer of the cerebrum that is involved in control of coordination, sensation, and motor activity.

Cerebrum The uppermost part of the brain that is largely responsible for conscious mental processes, or thought.

Chromosome Cell structure that contains the hereditary information in the form of DNA.

Clone An exact genetic copy of an organism.

COMT An enzyme that breaks down dopamine in the substantia nigra.

Corpus striatum A small part of the brain that receives dopamine signals from the substantia nigra; involved in control of movement, balance, and walking.

Cytoplasm The material inside a cell which includes the cytosol (the fluid inside the cell membrane or wall) and the organelles.

Dementia Loss of intellectual ability and/or memory, usually due to a degenerative neurological disease, such as Alzheimer's.

Dendrites Branching extensions of a neuron that receive impulses from other nerve cells and carry them toward the cell body.

DNA   Deoxyribonucleic acid; the nucleic acid found in the chromosomes that contains the hereditary information.

Dominant gene   A gene whose trait is expressed (appears in the organism) whenever the gene is present, even if there is only one copy of the gene in the individual.

Dopamine   A neurotransmitter released in the brain by the substantia nigra; involved in control of movement, balance, and walking.

Dyskinesia   The involuntary and uncontrollable flowing movement of limbs and body that results from taking levodopa to treat Parkinson's disease.

Embryo   The earliest stage of life, from the fertilized egg to differentiation of stem cells to form organs and tissues.

Embryonic stem cell   The cells in a blastocyst that are undifferentiated and are capable of becoming any type of body cell.

Enzyme   A protein that acts as a catalyst, or activator, of a specific chemical reaction.

Gene   A specific sequence of DNA nucleotides that controls the synthesis of a specific protein.

Genetic   Referring to genes or inheritance through genes.

Genome   An organism's or species' complete set of genes.

Heredity   The passing from parents to offspring of genetic material and the traits they specify.

Impulse   A chemical and electrical signal that travels between neurons.

In vitro fertilization   Union of the sperm and egg in a laboratory dish, outside the mother's body.

Inherit   Referring to the genes and traits that are passed from parents to offspring.

Involuntary   Not under voluntary control by the individual.

L-dopa See levodopa.

Levodopa An amino acid that is a precursor to dopamine; used to treat Parkinson's disease.

Lewy body A round collection of material that forms and accumulates inside certain brain cells, especially in the substantia nigra, in people suffering from Parkinson's disease.

Metabolism All the chemical reactions that take place in a living organism.

Micrographia A symptom of Parkinson's disease in which handwriting becomes smaller and smaller as the disease progresses.

Mitochondria Cell organelles that break down nutrients, usually glucose, for energy.

Molecule The smallest unit of an element or compound; consists of one or more atoms.

Monoamine oxidase B (MAO-B) An enzyme that breaks down dopamine after it is released by substantia nigra neurons.

Mutation An error in the order of nucleotides in a gene or an abnormality in chromosome structure or number.

Neurologist A medical doctor who specializes in diseases of the nervous system.

Neuron A nerve cell; the type of cell that carries impulses through the nervous system.

Neurotransmitter A chemical released by neurons that stimulates impulses in the adjacent neurons.

Neurotrophic hormones Hormones that facilitate the growth and health of neurons.

Nucleotides The chemical building blocks of DNA and RNA; consist of a sugar, phosphate group, and one of four nitrogen-containing bases.

Nucleus The control center of the cell; contains the hereditary material DNA.

Organelle A very small structure within a cell that is the site of a particular cell function.

Oxidation A chemical reaction that involves oxygen combining with some material to make a new substance.

Oxidative stress Excess oxidation of substances that may occur in cells.

Parkinsonism A condition that is not true Parkinson's disease but that presents with many or all Parkinson's symptoms.

Parkinson's disease A disorder that affects nerve cells in the substantia nigra, a section of the brain that controls movement and balance.

Pesticide A chemical, usually synthetic, that is used to kill agricultural pests, especially insects. Exposure to pesticides may contribute to Parkinson's symptoms.

Polymorphism A condition in which there is more than one normal form of a gene.

Receptor The part of a neuron or other cell that has sites able to receive chemical signals from other cells.

Recessive gene A gene whose trait is expressed (appears) only if the offspring has two genes for the trait, one from each parent.

Replication The copying of DNA and RNA molecules in chromosomes.

Ribonucleic acid (RNA) A single-stranded molecule that functions in protein synthesis by carrying information from DNA to ribosomes, which generate proteins.

Ribosomes Structures in a cell nucleus that translate genes to create proteins.

Rigidity Stiffness and/or immobility of a limb, part of the body, or the whole body; a symptom of Parkinson's disease.

Spinal cord The thick "rope" of nerves that runs from the brain and down the back; the spinal cord is covered by bone (the spinal column) and has nerves that extend from it to all parts of the body.

Striatum See corpus striatum.

Stem cell A cell that is capable of differentiating to become another, specific type of body cell.

Substantia nigra A structure in the brain that is the primary producer and releaser of dopamine and that is involved in the control of movement and balance.

Synapse The fluid-filled gap between neurons.

Transcription The exact copying of DNA prior to cell division.

Tremors Shaking or trembling in a part of the body.

Tyrosine An amino acid that is in food and is also a precursor to production of dopamine and adrenaline.

Voluntary muscle A muscle that can be moved at will.

BIBLIOGRAPHY

Ahlskog, J. Eric. *The Parkinson's Disease Treatment Book*. New York: Oxford University Press, 2005.

Blake-Krebs, Barbara, and Linda Herman. *When Parkinson's Strikes Early*. Alameda, Calif.: Hunter House, 2001.

Bonifati, Vincenzo. "The LRRK2-G2019S Mutation: Opening a Novel Era in Parkinson's Disease Genetics," The Michael J. Fox Foundation for Parkinson's Research Web site. Available online. URL: http://www.michaeljfox.org/news/article. php?id=234.

Duvoisin, Roger C., and Jacob Sage. *Parkinson's Disease: A Guide for Patient and Family*. Philadelphia: Lippincott Williams & Wilkins, 2001.

Fox, Michael J. *Lucky Man*. New York: Hyperion, 2002.

Havemann, Joel. *A Life Shaken: My Encounter with Parkinson's Disease*. Baltimore: Johns Hopkins University Press, 2002.

Mayo Clinic Press Release. "Strong Evidence of a Genetic Risk Factor for Parkinson's Disease," The Michael J. Fox Foundation for Parkinson's Research Web site. Available online. URL: http://www.michaeljfox.org/news/article.php?id=239.

Parkinson, James. "An Essay on the Shaking Palsy," Journal of Neuropsychiatry & Clinical Neurosciences Web site. Available online. URL: http://neuro.psychiatryonline.org/cgi/content/full/14/2/223.

"Researchers Grow Neural, Blood Vessel Cells from Adult Stem Cells," The Michael J. Fox Foundation for Parkinson's Research Web site. Available online. URL: http://www.michaeljfox.org/news/article.php?id=260.

Reuters. "Studies Line Up on Parkinson's-Pesticides Link." Scientific American Web site. URL: www.sciam.com/article.cfm?alias=studies-line-up-on-parkin&chanID=sa003.

Silverstein, Alvin, et al. *Parkinson's Disease.* Berkeley Heights, N.J: Enslow, 2002.

Transcript of Testimony by Michael J. Fox before the Senate Appropriations Committee, September 14, 2000. CNN.com Transcripts Web site. Available online. URL: http://transcripts.cnn.com/TRANSCRIPTS/0009/14/se.03.html.

Weiner, William, J., et al. *Parkinson's Disease: A Complete Guide for Patients and Families.* Baltimore: Johns Hopkins University Press, 2001.

Wiederholt, Wigbert C. *Neurology for Non-Neurologists.* Philadelphia: WB Saunders, 2000.

FURTHER READING

Blake-Krebs, Barbara, and Linda Herman. *When Parkinson's Strikes Early*. Berkeley, Calif.: Hunter House, 2001.

Fox, Michael J. *Lucky Man*. New York: Hyperion, 2002.

Havemann, Joel. *A Life Shaken: My Encounter with Parkinson's Disease*. Baltimore: Johns Hopkins University Press, 2004.

Hunt-Christensen, Jackie. *The First Year—Parkinson's Disease*. New York: Marlowe, 2005.

Peterman-Schwarz, Shelley. *Parkinson's Disease: 300 Tips for Making Life Easier*. New York: Demos Medical, 2006.

Silverstein, Alvin, et al. *Parkinson's Disease*. Berkeley Heights, N.J.: Enslow, 2002.

Weiner, William, J., et al. *Parkinson's Disease: A Complete Guide for Patients and Families*. Baltimore: Johns Hopkins University Press, 2001.

WEB SITES

The Brain Matters: American Academy of Neurology
http://www.thebrainmatters.org
This site provides information prepared by neurologists to help readers understand common disorders of the brain.

The Michael J. Fox Foundation for Parkinson's Research
http://www.michaeljfox.org
Michael J. Fox's official Web site informs readers about Parkinson's research and other current issues about the disease.

National Institute of Neurological Disorders and Stroke
http://www.ninds.nih.gov
New stories, articles, and research information can be found at
   this site sponsored by the National Institutes of Health.

National Parkinson Foundation
http://www.parkinson.org
The National Parkinson Foundation's Web site provides infor-
   mation about news and events that affect the research and
   development of Parkinson's disease, as well as giving readers
   access to its quarterly newsletter, The Parkinson Report.

Parkinson's Action Network
http://www.parkinsonsaction.org
This Web site is sponsored by the Parkinson's Action Network.
   This site provides information about funding for and legisla-
   tion that affects the research and treatment of Parkinson's
   disease.

Parkinson's Disease Foundation
http://www.pdf.org
At this Web site, the Parkinson's Disease Foundation provides
   information about research, education, and public advo-
   cacy for the cure of Parkinson's disease. News articles and
   reports on research give readers a better understanding of
   the disease.

PICTURE CREDITS

INDEX

ABOUT THE AUTHOR

Natalie Goldstein is a longtime science writer. She has master's degrees in education and science and has written several science books for children and young adults. She has also written extensively on science and health for publishers of textbooks for students in elementary school, middle school, and high school.